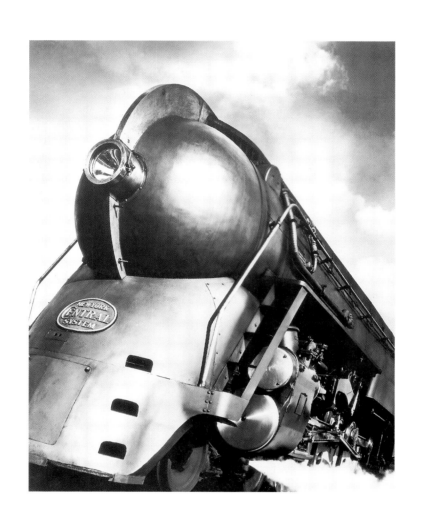

20th

CENTURY LIMITED

KARL ZIMMERMANN

MBI Publishing Company

First published in 2002 by MBI Publishing Company, Galtier Plaza, Suite 200, 380 Jackson Street, St. Paul, MN 55101-3885 USA.

© Andover Junction Publications, 2002

Book design and editing by Mike Schafer, Andover Junction Publications, Lee, Ill., and Blairstown, N.J. Layout by Kevin J. Holland, type&DESIGN, Burlington, Ontario. Technical production by Jim Popson, Andover Junction Publications. Editorial assistant, Wendy Yegoiants.

Cover design by Tom Heffron, MBI Publishing Company.

MBI Publishing books are also available at discounts in bulk quantity for industrial or sales-promotional use. For details, write to Special Sales Manager at Motorbooks International Wholesalers & Distributors, Galtier Plaza, Suite 200, 380 Jackson Street, St. Paul, MN 55101-3885 USA.

Library of Congress Cataloging-in-Publication data available

ISBN: 0-7603-1422-5

Front cover: In this heroic view from 1940, the westbound *20th Century Limited* roars under the Bear Mountain Bridge at Manitou, N.Y., and through the Highlands of the Hudson, by far the most scenic part of the train's run. It's June 16, close to the longest day of the year, so the passengers will be able to enjoy the river views all the way to Albany. A streamlined Hudson-type locomotive, Class J3a No. 5451 delivered by Alco in April 1938, is laying back a light plume of coal smoke in a manner that bespeaks speed. THE EDWARD L. MAY MEMORIAL COLLECTION, COURTESY RICHARD STOVING

Frontispiece: Considered one of the finest examples of streamlined steam locomotives, the New York Central J-class Hudsons that were assigned to *20th Century Limited* service spoke of the future. Their streamstyling was the work of Henry Dreyfuss, and though the reign of these racy locomotives was relatively short—less than a decade—they became an icon for a world-famous train that served the New York–Chicago market for 65 years. NEW YORK CENTRAL, PHIL AND BEV BIRK COLLECTION

Title page: With Storm King Mountain and the storied Hudson River serving as a backdrop, the 1948 edition of the *20th Century Limited* cruises southward through Cold Spring, N.Y., en route to New York City. NEW YORK CENTRAL, PETER V. TILP COLLECTION

Verso page: Morning sun glints off the silvery bullet nose of the Dreyfuss Hudson locomotive leading the eastbound *20th Century Limited* at Oscawanna, N.Y., in June 1940. HERBERT H. HARWOOD SR., HERBERT H. HARWOOD JR. COLLECTION

Contents page: Every passenger train worth its salt had a writing desk in the lounge, stocked with the train's own stationery. This letterhead that serves as the background for the contents listing carried the *Century*'s signature design element: repeating parallel bars spliced by the train name in stylish Art Deco lettering. JACK FERRY COLLECTION

Back cover, upper left: During the first hour of its overnight journey from Chicago to New York City, the *20th Century Limited* races through the sand-dune country of northwest Indiana in the mid-1960s. Late-afternoon sun casts a glow on the train's *Creek*-series observation car as travelers sip martinis and Manhattans. JIM BOYD

Back cover, upper right: The interior of observation car *Sandy Creek* in 1963 shows the simple, modern design of its solarium area. This and sister car *Hickory Creek* were built in 1948 and updated in 1962. ALAN BRADLEY

Back cover, lower right: There was a time when famous trains were prominently advertised in major periodicals, and the *Century* was a prime example. This ad from the *Saturday Evening Post* shows the 1938 edition of the train with its red carpet at New York's Grand Central Terminal. BILLS STRASSNER COLLECTION

Front end paper: Late on a June day in 1938, the new, streamlined version of the *20th Century Limited* speeds across the causeway northwest of Peekskill, N.Y., on a trial run up the Hudson River valley. ED NOWAK, NEW YORK CENTRAL, PETER V. TILP COLLECTION

Back end paper: Having photographed the scene of approaching trial-run *20th Century Limited* that appears as the front end paper of this book, New York Central photographer Ed Nowak turns around for this memorable scene of the train rapidly receding toward the setting sun. ED NOWAK, NEW YORK CENTRAL, PETER V. TILP COLLECTION

Printed in China

CONTENTS

20TH CENTURY LIMITED

NEW YORK CENTRAL SYSTEM

ACKNOWLEDGMENTS

If Pennsylvania Railroad's *Broadway Limited* was a train of the financial establishment, New York Central's competing *20th Century Limited* was a train of the stars. Actress Gloria Swanson waves to her fans from the observation platform of the *Century* at New York's Grand Central Terminal on August 17, 1931. NEW YORK CENTRAL

As this book on the *20th Century Limited* developed, the expected cast of generous and knowledgeable old friends stepped up to help as they have in the past, and new friends have swelled their ranks.

Simply reading the credit lines throughout this volume will show how instrumental to this project Peter V. Tilp has been in sharing his fine collection of photographs and brochures. As I've come to expect, Bill Howes provided not only priceless materials but also a wealth of knowledge. Joe Welsh was hugely helpful as I mapped out my research. Bob Schmidt, Herb Harwood, Bill Middleton, Dave Randall, Phil and Bev Birk, Bill Strassner, Kevin Holland, Mike McBride, Chuck Newton, Cal's Classics' Bill Caloroso, Jack Ferry, and William Raia generously opened their collections. Don Wood, George Speir, Andrew M. Spieker, Jim Boyd, Alan Bradley, Gerald Brimacombe, John Dziobko, Jim Shaughnessy, and Hoang Chi Cook provided their own photography. Important photographs also came from the Edward L. May Memorial Collection, courtesy of Richard Stoving, DeGolyer Library at Southern Methodist University, and the Otto Perry Collection at the Western History Department of the Denver Public Library.

The Foreword appeared in slightly different form in *Trains* Magazine; permission to incorporate it here is appreciated. Other material is drawn from various stories of mine in *Passenger Train Journal*.

A considerable body of literature surrounds the *20th Century Limited*; among the books I found the most helpful in retelling the story of this great train are Edward Hungerford's *The Run of the Twentieth Century*, Lucius Beebe's *20th Century*, and Arthur Dubin's *Some Classic Trains* and *More Classic Trains*.

Finally, I thank Mike Schafer of Andover Junction Publications for his good work—as editor, designer, godfather, collaborator—in bringing this book to fruition. Without his participation, it would have been a far different (and far poorer) volume.

—*Karl Zimmermann*

FACING PAGE: Insulated from the outside elements and the needless haste of the jet age, passengers aboard the *20th Century Limited* enjoy cocktails in the Lookout Lounge of a *Creek*-series sleeper-observation car. It's dusk at Harmon, N.Y., in the mid-1960s, and the westbound streamliner is pausing for the obligatory electric-to-diesel locomotive change. The end of such civilized, exclusive travel between New York and Chicago is only months away. KARL ZIMMERMANN

A TRAIN THAT DEFINED A CENTURY

f ever a train and an era were meant for each other, New York Central's *20th Century Limited* and its eponymous century were that match. Images and associations triggered by this impeccable train with the inspired name pour out, a rich flood that washes through the decades.

There's the red carpet rolled out for departure, the magnates and movie stars, the extra fare, the all-Pullman (and later all-private-room) exclusivity, the elegant Hudson locomotives (both standard and streamlined) and, later, the two-tone

Considered by many transportation historians to be "the perfect train," New York Central's 1938 edition of the *20th Century Limited*—the first streamlined version—marches out of Chicago's La Salle Street Station in late summer 1938. Leading the ultra-exclusive two-tone gray streamliner is one of the Central's knife-prow J-class Hudson-type locomotives whose styling was the work of industrial designer Henry Dreyfuss. ED NOWAK, NEW YORK CENTRAL; PETER V. TILP COLLECTION

Twentieth Century Limited leaving Chicago

gray, lightning-striped diesels. Think "Great Steel Fleet." Think "Water Level Route—You Can Sleep," green marker lights for multi-section operations, head-to-head races with Pennsylvania Railroad's *Broadway Limited* on Chicago's South Side. Think "Only 16 hours, New York to Chicago," and remember Henry Dreyfuss' ultimately stylish, exquisitely posh streamlining, and, finally, *Hickory Creek* and *Sandy Creek*, the deep-windowed observation cars of the train's final, postwar expression.

The *20th Century Limited*. What a grand name! And what a genius was the man who thought it up. He was George H. Daniels, New York Central's general passenger agent for nearly two decades (and before that, perhaps both significantly and ironically, a seller of patent medicine), father of the redcap, and the man who talked the postmaster general into placing New York Central's *Empire State Express* on a stamp. The *20th Century Limited* was his baby, and right from the moment the train hit the rails on June 15, 1902, it represented speed, luxury, and cachet—characteristics it would retain virtually up to the moment of its sudden demise on December 3, 1967. They're also characteristics that continued to fascinate Americans right to the end of the twentieth century— and into the next millennium.

The first years of that now-vanished century were an exhilarating and expansive time in passenger railroading, and Daniel's *20th Century Limited* was the

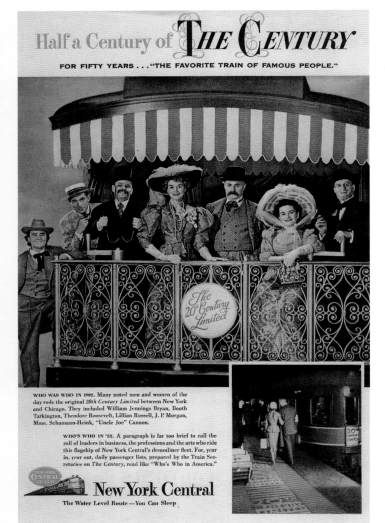

Half a Century of **THE CENTURY**

FOR FIFTY YEARS . . . "THE FAVORITE TRAIN OF FAMOUS PEOPLE."

WHO WAS WHO IN 1902. Many noted men and women of the day rode the original *20th Century Limited* between New York and Chicago. They included William Jennings Bryan, Booth Tarkington, Theodore Roosevelt, Lillian Russell, J. P. Morgan, Mme. Schumann-Heink, "Uncle Joe" Cannon.

WHO'S WHO IN '52. A paragraph is far too brief to call the roll of leaders in business, the professions and the arts who ride this flagship of New York Central's dreamliner fleet. For, year in, year out, daily passenger lists, prepared by the Train Secretaries on *The Century*, read like "Who's Who in America."

New York Central

The Water Level Route—You Can Sleep

10

perfect train for the moment, with the perfect name and, in Daniels, the perfect P. T. Barnum-like publicist. Few things are born into a vacuum, and the New York–Chicago *Century* evolved from the also luxurious *Lake Shore Limited*, inaugurated five years earlier in 1897. The *Century* shaved four hours from the *Lake Shore*'s running time, cutting it to an "experimental" 20 hours.

By 1902, George Pullman's Palace Car Company had gobbled up its Buffalo-based rival founded by Webster Wagner, initially New York Central's sleeping-car company of choice, so the *20th Century Limited* was a Pullman operation from the beginning. Pullman it would remain both in provenance of equipment and, until its last decade of operation, exclusivity of service. From the train's all-new wooden consists completed in 1904 (it had first used refurbished *Lake Shore* cars), to the various "heavyweight" or "standard" versions with the riveted steel cars introduced in 1910, right through the streamliners of 1938 and 1948, Pullman built virtually all the cars ever carried by this famous train, and they were unfailingly the most luxurious available. By the late 1920s, arguably this fine train's finest hour, this meant lots of cars—all sleepers, diners, and lounges, with nary a chair car sullying a *Century* consist until 1958—since multiple sections were the rule.

For all of the *Century*'s grandeur and dignity in the heavyweight, Pullman-green, open-observation-platform era, many remember the train best for its 1938 streamlined incarnation, a high-water mark of

Local residents have come down to Englewood station on Chicago's South Side on August 4, 1929, to watch the eastbound *Century* pause only a few minutes out of La Salle Street Station. Leading the train is Hudson No. 5230, in pristine condition for its important task of relaying the *Century* toward New York City. At left behind the well-wishers is the Pennsylvania Railroad's rival train, the *Broadway Limited*, also on its way to the East Coast. At the time of this scene, Englewood station catered to an exclusive neighborhood that generated much business for many of Chicago's trains. A. W. JOHNSON, PETER V. TILP COLLECTION

industrial design wrought by Henry Dreyfuss. Dreyfuss created a streamliner of understated yet unforgettable elegance. Its "cleanlined" design perfectly expressed the exhilarating speed that always had been among the train's signature features.

The designer's touch was ubiquitous. Outside, it was seen in the classy, cool color scheme—a blue-edged dark gray band on a background of lighter gray, with twin silver stripes at window level—and in the J3-class Hudson on the point, by acclamation the most successful steam-locomotive streamlining ever. The stylish interiors were all his too, as were crockery, napery, glassware, silver, menus, magazine covers, ashtrays, matchbooks, stationery, tickets, and much more. Most items carried the distinctive logo with repeated horizontal bars perhaps best known on the lighted observation-car tailsigns.

"Café Century," the dining car, offered seating in dinettes, banquettes, and other comfortable groupings typical of a fine restaurant. Food and service sustained the tradition of excellence solidly established in the heavyweight era. After dinner, the white linens were whisked off, replaced by rust-colored cloths. Bright lights were doused and soft, rosy ones cranked up, along with recorded swing music, as the car was transformed into a classy nightclub.

A brochure issued for the inauguration of the second streamlined version of the *Century* in 1948 featured full colored renderings that showcased the train's swank interior. As with the 1938 edition, Henry Dreyfuss styled the train inside and out. WILLIAM F. HOWES JR. COLLECTION

There were innovations beyond styling. The train's New York–Chicago timing was dropped to 16 hours flat, close to the fastest it would ever be. And, with then-novel enclosed roomettes replacing the traditional open sections, the *Century* became an all-private-room train, touted as a first.

It was a first—sort of, since simultaneously, on June 15, 1938, arch-competitor Pennsylvania Railroad had inaugurated a brand-new, streamlined, all-room *Broadway Limited*, styled by Dreyfuss rival Raymond Loewy. Throughout the *Century*'s history, in fact, it was shadowed by the *Broadway Limited* (and its predecessor, the *Pennsylvania Special*, inaugurated on the same day as the *Century*). Over the years, each improvement by the *Century* in timing or equipment was met by the *Broadway*. Even the final expression of the *Century*—the 1948 re-equipping, with the *Creek*-series observation cars—was echoed by its Pennsy counterpart. But for all its striving, the *Broadway* never could achieve the prestige, nor the ridership, of the *Century*.

In the railroad era, *20th Century Limited* was a household name for virtually every American, very much a part of the popular culture. Charles MacArthur and Ben Hecht (co-authors earlier of "The Front Page") in 1932 wrote "Twentieth Century," an engaging farce set at a train gate in Grand Central Terminal and aboard a heavyweight Pullman with sections and a lounge, all reproduced on stage with loving accuracy. In 1978 the play reappeared on Broadway as "On the Twentieth Century," a musical. This time the train was the 1938 streamliner, an Art Deco confection created by stage designer Robin Wagner in emulation (though not slavish) of

Dreyfuss' train. In one scene, Imogene Coca appeared splayed against the unmistakable nose of a streamlined J3 Hudson.

E. B. White wrote a poem about the *Century,* and Lucius Beebe a whole book. In 1930 New York Central published Edward Hungerford's *The Run of the Twentieth Century,* a heroic account of the train at its multi-section heavyweight height that reads like a romantic epic. Virtually every New York City and Chicago newspaper columnist took a look at the train, and rarely was heard a discouraging word.

Significantly, *20th Century Limited* is the only historic train name that Amtrak deemed too illustrious to appropriate, choosing instead *Lake Shore Limited*—the *Century's* predecessor and later humble running mate—for its New York–Chicago Water Level Route train. Although you still can ride the *California Zephyr, Empire Builder, Crescent, Sunset Limited* or *Wolverine* under Amtrak, you can board the *20th Century Limited* only in recollection or imagination. There, however, you can sashay with anticipation down a red carpet amid the bustle of well-dressed passengers and scurrying redcaps, pass an enticing observation car (either open-platform or boat-tailed, depending on your age or inclination), and settle down in a plush Pullman aboard the greatest train in the world—the benchmark against which all others were judged.

And now, looking back in admiration, we mark the train's most special and appropriate anniversary—its 100th. Had it survived, it would have been a century of the *Century.*

Karl Zimmermann
June 15, 2002

1

RIDING THE GREATEST TRAIN EVER MADE

Bursting through the revolving door into splashes of sun that snuck into the skyscraper canyon of Wall Street, Rudy Carpenter flagged down a cab. "Grand Central Station," he said. "I'm catching the *Century*."

The cabbie nodded, spun the taxi around, and headed for the West Side Drive. Rudy slipped his gold pocket watch from his vest.

Four forty-five—much earlier than he'd usually leave his office, but he didn't want to be late. Riding the streamlined *20th Century Limited*, which had been

With a 1948 re-equipping close at hand, the eastbound *20th Century Limited* rolls away from its South Side Chicago stop at Englewood, Ill. Still sharp after nearly a decade of service, this consist is basically the Dreyfuss-styled streamliner of 1938. Laid up during World War II, observation car *Pelee Island* on this day's train was rebuilt as a 4-double-bedroom buffet-lounge observation in 1946 (it previously had contained just one master room and one double bedroom) and returned to *Century* service. Though nearing replacement by deep-windowed *Creek*-series observations, the *Island* cars would continue to see service in extra sections of the *Century* and on the *Commodore Vanderbilt*, Central's second best New York-to-Chicago train. EDMUND SPIEKER

15

The *Magic Carpet* rolls out again

IT'S Century time! A minute ago, outside the station, you were in the heart of a great city, with crowds, blaring taxis, newsboys shouting the evening headlines. Now you're in a different world as you follow that crimson carpet down the platform of Grand Central Terminal toward the softly lighted, streamlined cars that will be your club on wheels for tonight.

RELAX BY TWILIGHT

Magically, the day's tension vanishes as you step into the Century's Observation Car. Easy chairs invite you to relax. And outside the wide windows, the twilit beauty of the Water Level Route unrolls a background for repose.

THE FACE IS FAMILIAR

There is a fascination about your "dinner of the Century." For nearby may be a face you last saw in technicolor, or one that would be news on any financial page.

AWAKE REFRESHED

You arrive at your best. For all night, in the quiet privacy of your room, a spacious bed, a rubber-foam mattress, and the smooth Water Level Route have conspired to give you deep, refreshing sleep.

The *only* all-room extra-fare train between New York and Chicago.

NEW YORK CENTRAL
The Water Level Route—You Can Sleep

20TH CENTURY LIMITED

all over the newspapers at its inaugural less than a year before, was an opportunity not to be missed.

This was May of 1939, a heady time when America was climbing out of the Depression's abyss and hadn't yet tumbled into the worse problems waiting in the guise of World War II, and New York City was buzzing. Towering ahead to the right as the taxi sped uptown was the Empire State Building, still something of a novelty in the skyline. Off to the left was the Hudson—or North River, as it was known to Rudy and others who came and went on the stylish ocean liners always present at the docks there. The river was blue-gray under a high sun. Colorful funnels showed the ownership of the liners scattered at the docks on both sides of the river. Looking across the water toward Hoboken, Rudy spotted the mustard-colored stacks of a ship he'd sailed on: North German Lloyd's *Bremen.*

Just before the taxi dropped down the ramp at 42nd Street, the three large black-and-red stacks of the French Line's majestic *Normandie* reared up. This ship was a speedster; in its five years it had twice seized the Blue Ribband for the fastest transatlantic crossing, though the *Queen Elizabeth* was the current holder. The *Normandie's* Art Deco interiors were the smartest, most stylish afloat. She was, in short, the *20th Century Limited* of the North Atlantic.

Carpenter's cab turned onto Vanderbilt Avenue, then ducked into the taxi drop-off area where dark-uniformed redcaps waited for luggage. "Roomette 5 in car 253," Carpenter said. With a nubby pencil, the redcap scribbled on a tag, tore the stub and handed it to Rudy, then threw the accountant's brown-leather valise on top of the growing stack of luggage on his cart. "The *Century's* on track 34," he said. "See you aboard."

Grand Central was familiar territory for Carpenter, but grasping the brass handle, worn smooth and shiny by countless thousands of hands, and entering the vast, stately concourse was always pleasing. (Actually, Rudy as often chose the trains of the Pennsylvania Railroad, archcompetitor of the Central, so he also knew well the neoclassical grandeur of Pennsylvania Station, some dozen blocks south and west.)

The four-faced golden clock atop Grand Central's information booth in mid concourse read 4:15, since railroads then ran on standard time, even in the summer when the populace marched to the daylight-saving's drummer. The cavernous, echoing hall was swarming with commuters hurrying for trains; they poured down the stairs, washing around him as he descended from the Vanderbilt entrance. They swirled in from the Graybar passageway, and from 42nd Street. Most were headed for the station's lower level, dedicated to suburban service, where they'd catch New York Central trains to Westchester County's bedroom communities and New York, New Haven & Hartford trains to Fairfield County's suburbia by Long Island Sound.

On the upper level, the Central's "Great Steel Fleet"—the long-distance expresses, with chair cars, Pullmans, diners, lounges, and observation cars—was in mid sailing. Already gone were the *Knickerbocker* for St. Louis; the *Commodore Vanderbilt,* second only to the *Century* on the Chicago route; the *Advance Commodore Vanderbilt,* also all-Pullman; and the *Ohio State Limited* to Cincinnati. Lined up to leave five minutes behind the *Century,* "on its markers," as railroaders would say in reference to the marker lamps displayed on the rear of all trains, was the *Pacemaker,* a deluxe coach train for Chicago. Later would come the *Wolverine,* also to Chicago but via the Michigan Central route north of Lake Erie, the *Lake Shore Limited* to Chicago, the Pullman-only *Detroiter,* the *Southwestern Limited* to St. Louis, the *Cleveland Limited,* the *Ontarian-Lake Erie* to Cleveland and to Toronto, the *Niagara* to Niagara Falls, and—operated jointly with the Delaware & Hudson Railroad—the Pullman-only *Montreal Limited.*

This ad for the 1938 *Century* highlights many of the aspects of the train that made it special: the red carpet, interwoven with the famous Dreyfuss-designed logo, that was rolled out at Grand Central Terminal; "The Water Level Route" on which "You Can Sleep"; the celebrities who might be riding the train.
KARL ZIMMERMANN COLLECTION

From Grand Central Terminal that evening, Pullman cars would fan out all over the East and Midwest, ending their runs at Albany, Boston, Buffalo, Burlington, Chicago, Cincinnati, Cleveland, Detroit, Fort Edward, Grand Rapids, Lake Placid, Malone, Massena, Montreal, Niagara Falls, Ogdensburg, Oswego, Plattsburg, Rochester, Rutland, Saginaw-Bay City, St. Louis, Syracuse, Toronto, Utica, Watertown, and Worcester. These were not just cities served by Pullman cars, but places where they terminated—and where berths could be occupied after arrival until a reasonable rising time, should those arrivals be in the wee hours. Rudy had ridden a number of them.

The list from Pennsylvania Station was even more imposing. Sleepers would leave to tie up at Akron, Asheville, Atlanta, Augusta, Baltimore, Birmingham, Boston, Charlotte, Chicago, Cincinnati, Cleveland, Detroit, Ellsworth, Farmington, Hot Springs, Knoxville, Louisville, Memphis, Miami, Nashville, New Orleans, Norfolk, Pittsburgh, Plymouth, Portland, Raleigh-Durham, Richmond, Roanoke, Rockland, Savannah, Shreveport, St. Louis, St. Petersburg, Tampa-Sarasota, Washington, Waterville, Wheeling, White Sulphur Springs, Wilmington, Winston-Salem, and Venice. If you were headed for any one of these

Grand Central Terminal—the official name of the splendid Beaux-Arts structure completed in 1913—was called "Grand Central Station" by most New Yorkers, and the name became a synonym for business and bustle. By any name it was a splendid place to begin a journey of consequence. Sunlight flooding through its huge windows (as in this 1941 view) became iconic, as did the round information booth with its four-faced clock that still stands in the concourse.
LIBRARY OF CONGRESS

destinations, you could board a train in midtown New York at a convenient evening hour and disembark the next day after a good night's sleep. And, taking a ferry across the Hudson River opened up another array of options: Pullmans operated by the Delaware, Lackawanna & Western, the Erie Railroad, the Central Railroad of New Jersey, the Lehigh Valley, and the Baltimore & Ohio.

But of all these Pullmans bound for all these places, none were as illustrious as the *20th Century Limited*'s streamlined Pullman sleepers, among them the one Rudy Carpenter was about to call "home" for the next 17 hours or so.

A queue was already building at track 34 by the time he got there: men in dark business suits and smartly dressed women in tailored clothes. The gateman arrived and spun the crank that scrolled the white-lettered black canvas destination sign into place: 20TH CENTURY LIMITED. PULLMANS ONLY. CHICAGO. He snapped on the light illuminating the track number, then pushed open the gate.

Rudy pulled his ticket envelope from his inside coat pocket and handed it to the conductors standing behind a tall portable check-in desk.

Both wore vested blue-black uniforms with brass buttons and gold watch chains draped across their bellies and round, billed, can-style hats. Hat badges identified one as the New York Central conductor, who collected—"lifted" in the argot of the trade—Rudy's transportation ticket, and the other as the Pullman conductor, who took his Pullman ticket and checked him off on the diagram sheet for the all-roomette car, one of nine sleeping cars carried by the *Century* that night.

Down the platform the *Century* shone in the subterranean gloom: a seemingly unbroken tube of light gray cars with dark gray window band edged in blue, accented with aluminum striping. Windows glowed softly, and smooth steel flanks glinted yellow with ambient light. It was the first streamliner Rudy had ever seen.

He joined the flow of passengers trailing down the long strip of red carpet, rolled out daily for this train's departure and for no other's, ever, anywhere. The first thing he glimpsed up close was the rounded end of an elegant observation car, with a distinctive *20th Century Limited* tail-sign, an Art Deco motif with stacked horizontal bars that was also woven into the red carpet. He peered through the windows and saw passengers already ensconced in the lounge, reading their afternoon papers. As he walked by the car, he read *Bedloes Island* from its gray flank and, on the letterboard, PULLMAN.

He walked by more Pullmans—*Imperial Falls, Imperial Highlands, Dutchess County*—and on past two diners, then still more Pullmans. At each vestibule, a porter stood ready to welcome passengers aboard. Rudy checked the car "loading numbers" shining in the windows near the doors until, almost at the head of the train, he found his: 253, a car called *City of Toledo*, which held 17 roomettes.

"Good afternoon, sir." Smart-looking in his dark-blue, dressy "station jacket," the porter took Rudy's overnight bag and led him into the coolness and gentle hum of air conditioning aboard the sleeper, then

Number 25, the westbound *Century*, has left Grand Central some 20 minutes earlier and is swinging around a bend in the Harlem River at Marble Hill as it approaches Spuyten Duyvil. The T-motor is about ten miles into its 33-mile run to Harmon, where the third-rail, direct-current electrification ends. The picture is taken from the bridge carrying Broadway (an avenue associated with rival Pennsylvania Railroad and its flagship train) over the Harlem River and New York Central's main line. E. L. DE GOLYER JR. PHOTOGRAPH COLLECTION, SOUTHERN METHODIST UNIVERSITY, DALLAS, TEXAS; COLLECTION NO. AG1982.232:24375

The handoff at Harmon from electric to steam and later diesel power for the *Century* began in early 1907 with the first operation of locomotive-hauled trains over the new electrification and continued throughout the train's career. Here, "motor" T3a No. 277 has pulled in from Grand Central and will turn over its train to a streamlined J3a for the 257-mile run to Syracuse. Locomotives will be changed again at Buffalo and Toledo. L. W. RICE, HERBERT H. HARWOOD JR. COLLECTION

down the narrow corridor to roomette 5. The porter stowed Rudy's overnight bag, then took his straw summer hat, slipped it into a paper bag designed for this purpose, and stacked it with the satchel. About then the redcap arrived, lugging Rudy's large suitcase. He stowed it under the seat in the roomette and discreetly pocketed his tip.

Rudy lived with his parents in their substantial clapboard home in Passaic, New Jersey. His train-happy ten-year-old nephew, who also lived there much of the time, had begged him to pay close attention so he could recount all the details of this wonderful new streamliner. Since departure was many minutes away, Rudy stepped out again briefly onto the platform and walked forward to see the rest of the train. He passed *Century Inn*; looking through that car's windows, he saw a cozy, clublike lounge and, farther along, a barber shop. Next he passed a workaday baggage-mail car, noticing the slot in the car's side where he could post a letter if he chose. ("TR. 25," the postmark would read, "N.Y.–Chicago, R.P.O.," for Railway Post Office.) On the head end was a boxy electric locomotive, an aesthetic mismatch with the clean, sleek lines of the cars. He knew that the electric's stint would be a short one, as streamlined steam would take over at Harmon, just 33 miles up the Hudson.

Back on board, Rudy examined his roomette—another first for him, since this style of accommodation was only then being popularized hand-in-hand with streamliners as an alternative to the curtain-draped open sections—facing seats during the day that transformed into upper and lower berths for night travel—that had been the norm for travelers of Rudy's generation. Undeniably small, the roomette was a marvel of compactness and engineering ingenuity, and it was truly private. A control panel held switches to adjust the fan and air conditioning and to turn on mirror, ceiling, reading, and night lights. Rudy pulled down the basin, filled it with hot water, stripped the blue-and-white wrapper marked "Pullman" off a little bar of Ivory soap, and washed up.

Then he made his way the length of the train through the immediate pre-departure bustle—late-arriving passengers scurrying down the platform with anxious glances at their watches, redcaps swinging the last bags aboard, porters slamming the Dutch doors to the vestibules. In the observation lounge at the train's hind end, in contrast, all was cool, soft silence, with the loudest sounds the rustle of afternoon newspaper or the clink of ice cubes in a glass.

"Anyone sitting there?"

"No, help yourself." A well-manicured gentleman in gray pinstripes cleared away the sports and business sections of the *Journal-American* and invited Rudy to sit. The observation car was filling quickly, so Rudy was happy to find a seat in the rear, solarium section, where the viewing seemed exceptionally good. He looked around with interest. To his way of thinking, the car epitomized the train's modernity, with decor truly Machine Age in inspiration. Predominant colors were blues and grays; designs were spare, even stark, with smooth curves predominating. On the bulkhead that separated the solarium from the main lounge was a recessed, glass-fronted case with a model of a J3a Hudson—the streamlined steam locomotive, powerful and fleet, that would take over at Harmon where electrified running ended. Above the model was a speedometer, *de rigueur* for observation cars.

"A Manhattan, please." From the enclosed service buffet forward came the rattle of a cocktail shaker, and in no time the Filipino attendant who had taken Rudy's order emerged with a tawny drink, anchored by a bright red cherry. As Rudy took his first sip, the sweetness of vermouth smoothing the bite of whiskey, the train nudged into motion. The platform with its red carpet slipped quickly behind, and the observation car swung gently from side to side as the *Century* nosed through the maze of switches at the throat of the terminal tracks, then plunged into the darkness of the Park Avenue Tunnel.

Within minutes the train burst into daylight, climbing to the elevated trackage above Harlem's busy sidewalks. After passing the 125th Street station, the *Century* crossed the Harlem River before following it to Spuyten Duyvil, where the tracks turned north along the Hudson. Late afternoon sun flooded the solarium and its well-dressed assemblage of readers, sightseers, and tipplers. Across the river the cliffs of the Palisades were dark in shadow. Through the rear windows Rudy watched the four-track main line reel off in a blur of crossties. The speedometer's needle now began to climb in earnest. Heavyweight multiple-unit electric trains slowing for stops at Riverdale, Dobbs Ferry, and other commuter destinations were left in the *Century*'s dust.

By the time the sun had dropped behind Bear Mountain and its eponymous suspension bridge was looming overhead, Rudy had made his way to the pair of dining cars located midtrain—cars unlike any Rudy had ever seen. For one thing, they had windows in the dining-room ends, so he could look from one car right into the next. For another, tables of varying sizes and shapes were asymmetrically arranged, a plan significantly different from the lockstep rows of square tables for four that he had encountered in other diners. Instead there was a mixture of tables for four or two, all laid with snowy white linen and substantial hotel-grade silverware. The steward in Café Century seated him at a table for two, handed him a menu, and set a meal check and pencil on the table. "Waiters are not permitted to take verbal orders" was printed pointedly across the check. There on the menu was that eye-catching logo he had seen on the observation car's tailsign and on the red carpet. It was replicated in subtle gray on the handsome china, on the matchbook that rested in the ashtray, everywhere.

"Lobster Newburg," Rudy wrote on the check, after due deliberation that had also taken into account the Planked Spring Lamb Steak *20th*

A lack of dents in the pilot of an absolutely clean J-class 4-6-4 pulling a likewise unsullied train suggest that that this scene was recorded very early in the life of the new streamliner, shown drifting westbound into Peekskill, N.Y. ED NOWAK, NEW YORK CENTRAL, HERBERT H. HARWOOD JR. COLLECTION

Century. The waiter tore off the top copy of the check, then headed for the kitchen to place the order. Before long he set the steaming, savory Newburg in front of Rudy, who made short work of it, and the pie á la mode that followed. By the time the *Century* had reached Albany, Rudy was back in the observation car, sipping cognac, smoking a cigar, and chatting with a Chicago-bound businessman.

"I'm not supposed to be here," Rudy confided. "The managing partner at my firm issued a directive: no travel on extra-fare trains. But I wanted to try the *Century*, so I decided I'd go ahead and pay the difference myself. Rudy chuckled. "He wasn't happy about it, but what could he say?"

Conversation in the observation car dwindled as passengers drifted off to bed. Rudy headed for his roomette, walking through the corridors of the sleepers, silent save for the muted thrumming of wheels on rails. Signs hanging in the corridors of each sleeper swung gently with the motion of the train: QUIET IS REQUESTED FOR THE BENEFIT OF THOSE WHO HAVE RETIRED.

Passing through the diners after the dinner hour, Rudy was startled by their transformation. The bright lights had been doused and an auxiliary system turned on, bathing the room in a soft, rosy glow. Rust-colored linens had replaced white. Swing music played—from a radio, Rudy surmised, or perhaps a phonograph—and some couples danced, though more sat in quiet conversation at the tables. He felt a pang of loneliness as he walked through the impromptu nightclub.

Back in his roomette, Rudy donned his pajamas. A big man, he was pleased with the ease of changing clothes in his own private room and made the inevitable comparison to the labored awkwardness of trying to get in and out of shirt and trousers horizontally, flopping around in an upper or lower berth. Ready for bed, he opened the door and zipped the curtains to cover the doorway. Contained by the curtains, he grasped a handle midway up the wall of the roomette, backed out part way

into the hall, and lowered the bed, which filled the room when latched into place. The bed was neatly made, with a brown Pullman blanket stretched taut.

Rudy slid under the covers. He raised the shade, then snapped off both ceiling and reading lights. He pushed the toggle switch over to "Nite," and the room was flooded with soft blue light. Out in the darkness, a small western New York city—Lyons, perhaps, or Newark—flashed by in a blur of lights. From just a few car-lengths ahead, the melodic whistle of the Hudson that had taken over at Harmon sounded again and again as the *Century* roared through the night. The soft clickety-clack below and the soothing rush of conditioned air offered a lullaby. Before long, Rudy dropped off to sleep.

He was nudged awake by the unnatural stillness. The *Century*, which, Rudy knew, wasn't scheduled for a station stop between Buffalo (not long past midnight) and the outskirts of Chicago, had paused in its westerly rush, interrupting the long-running rumble of wheel on rail. He raised his window shade on an empty platform, with pools of yellow light spilling from hooded lamps. "Toledo," he read, then felt a light bump of an engine coupling onto the train.

Almost immediately, two muted whistle blasts came from the head end, and the scene outside the window began to move, slipping backward

A LA CARTE

SOUPS, JUICES and COCKTAILS

Pot-Au-Feu-Fermiere, Cup .... .25	Fresh Shrimp Cocktail Lorenzo........ .45
Tureen .... .35	Clam Bouillon, Hot or Cold .... .25
Consomme, Hot, Cup .... .30	Clam Juice Cocktail................. .25
Jellied Consomme, Cup............. .35	Tomato Juice Cocktail............... .30
Fresh Fruit Cup .... .35	Two-Tone Cocktail .... .30
Chilled Prune Juice .... .25	Chilled Tomato Juice................ .25

Canapes of Anchovy-Shrimp.......... .65

ENTREES

Oven Baked Beans (Hot or Cold),	Grilled French Sardines, Sliced Tomatoes,
Brown Bread .50	Toasted Whole Wheat Bread........ .75
Genuine Russian Caviar on Toast......1.00	Broiled Lamb Chops (2), with Potatoes .1.10
Fried or Broiled Spring Chicken (Half),	Roast Prime Ribs of Beef with Potatoes..1.15
with Potatoes 1.10	Imported Frankfurters (Hot or Cold),
Minute Steak Grilled with Potatoes....1.35	Potato Salad .... .70
Small Sirloin Steak with Potatoes......1.75	Eggs—Boiled, Fried or Scrambled...... .35
Broiled Ham or Bacon............... .70	Poached on Toast .... .40
Half Portion...... .35	Omelettes—Plain .... .50
Broiled Ham or Bacon with Eggs...... .70	Parsley or Jelly................... .65
Fresh Fish, with Potatoes............. .95	Chopped Ham or Bacon........... .65
	Royal Mushroom Omelette............ .65

(Charcoal used exclusively for broiling)

Fried Robbins Island Oysters,	The Famous N.Y.C. Oyster Stew
Cole Slaw, Chili Sauce, Potatoes .65	or Little Neck Clam Stew .. .65

VEGETABLES

Vegetable Combination with	New Wax Beans in Cream or Fermiere. .35
Poached Egg .... .85	Potatoes—Mashed .... .20
Carrots and Peas.................... .25	Julienne, Argentine, O'Brien or
New Beets Fermiere................. .25	Lyonnaise........... .25
New Brussels Sprouts with Crumbs..... .35	Royal Mushrooms on Toast........... .45

DESSERTS

Individual Lemon Cream Pie.......... .30	Grape Fruit on Ice, Half....... .30
Plum Pudding, 20th Century Sauce.... .25	Stewed Prunes .... .30
French Pancakes with	Preserved Figs with Cream........... .35
Orange Marmalade .... .35	Apricots, Pears or Pineapple in Syrup.. .25
French Vanilla Ice Cream............. .25	N.Y.C. Baked Apple with Cream...... .25
Hot Chocolate Fudge Sundae.......... .35	
Orange 15; Sliced 25	Orange Juice, Iced .25
Sliced Bananas with Cream 30	Assorted Cookies 15 Extracted Honey 25
	Orange Marmalade 25

CHEESE

Liederkranz........... .40	Camembert... .40	Roquefort .... .40

(Toasted Hard or Soft Biscuits served with above Cheese orders)

Cream Cheese with Toasted Rye Bread, Wild Grape Jelly 35

COLD SUGGESTIONS, SALADS, ETC.

Stuffed Olives 35	Ripe or Green Olives 25	French Sardines in Olive Oil 60
Celery Hearts, Iced 35; Stuffed with Roquefort Cheese 50		Sliced Chicken, Tomato Surpris 1 00
Fresh Shrimp Salad 90		Roast Prime Ribs of Beef, Potato Salad 1.15
Sliced Smoked Tongue, Potato Salad 85		Cold Country Ham, Mexican Salad 85
Combination Salad 45 Potato Salad 30	Lettuce 35	Lettuce and Tomato 40 Sliced Tomatoes 35
Pineapple Salad, 20th Century, French Dressing 50		Chicken Salad 90 Chiffonade Salad 35
Mexican Salad 30 Roquefort Dressing 25	Thousand Island Dressing 15	Mayonnaise Dressing 15

BREAD, ETC.

Toast, Dry or Buttered 15	White, Whole Wheat or Rye Bread 15
Cream Toast 45 Milk Toast 30	French Toast with Jelly or Honey 40
Ry-Krisp 15 Crackers 10	Yeast Cake 10

COFFEE, TEA, ETC.

N.Y.C. Special Coffee with Cream (Pot) 25	Coffee (Demi-tasse) 15	Kaffee Hag Coffee (Pot for One) 25
Orange Pekoe, India, English Breakfast, Oolong or Green Tea (Pot for One) 25		
Postum (Pot for One) 25	Sanka Coffee (Pot for One) 25	Cocoa (Pot for One) 25
Individual Milk 15	Malted Milk (Pot for One) 25	Buttermilk, Bottle 15

Prices are Quoted in United States Currency

Chgo.   B. J. Bohlender, Manager Dining Service, New York

THE 20th CENTURY SALAD BOWL
Ry-Krisp
(Per Person)
60 Cents

For Sale
In U. S. A. Only

Martini Cocktail	.40
Manhattan Cocktail	.40
Old Fashioned Cocktail	.50
Creme de Menthe............	.50
Apricot Brandy	.50
Medoc	.50
Grand Marnier	.60
Benedictine	.60

Moselle Wine

1/4 Bottle, Imported........	1.50
American	.40

Rhine Wine

1/4 Bottle, Imported........	1.50

Sauterne

1/4 Bottle, Imported........	1.00
American	.40

Claret

1/4 Bottle, Imported........	1.00
American	.40

Riesling

1/4 Bottle, American........	.40

Domestic Ale or Beer .30

THE NEW 20th CENTURY DINNER
⊰ $1.75 ⊱

Chilled Celery Hearts

Spiced Pear	Radishes Rosette
Pimiento Olives	Ripe Olives

Pot-Au-Feu-Fermiere
Consomme Julienne or en Gelee

Clam Bouillon, Hot	Clam Juice Cocktail
Chilled Tomato Juice	Two-Tone Cocktail
Fresh Fruit Cup	Canape of Anchovy-Shrimp

Fresh Shrimp Cocktail Lorenzo

Broiled Lake Trout, Maitre d'Hotel
New Brussels Sprouts with Crumbs, Julienne Potatoes

Poached Eggs Benedict on Peanut Canape,
New Beets Fermiere, Argentine Potatoes

Planked Spring Lamb Steak, 20th Century, Carrots and Peas

Broiled Shrewsbury Squab, Guava Jelly, Timbale of Wild Rice,
Creamed Wax Beans, O'Brien Potatoes

Roast Prime Ribs of Beef, Au Jus
New Brussels Sprouts Polonaise, Lyonnaise Potatoes

> LOBSTER NEWBURG, 20th CENTURY,
> New Wax Beans Fermiere, Julienne Potatoes
> Served on this dinner $2.25

Romaine, Orange and Avocado, N.Y.C. Dressing

Peanut Muffins	Assorted Rolls	Lemon Raisin Sticks

Individual Lemon Cream Pie   Plum Pudding, 20th Century Sauce
French Pancakes with Orange Marmalade
Hot Chocolate Fudge Sundae
N.Y.C. Baked Apple with Cream   Grape Fruit on Ice, Half
or
Cream Cheese with Toasted Rye Bread, Wild Grape Jelly
Roquefort, Camembert or Liederkranz Cheese
with Toasted Biscuits

Tea	Individual Milk	N.Y.C. Special Coffee

Guests will please write on check each item desired.

---

toward New York City. Rudy glimpsed a streamlined Hudson standing wreathed in steam, no doubt the locomotive that had just come off his train. He watched trackside lights begin to blur as the rhythmic cadence of locomotive exhaust quickened, punctuated by more whistling. He could feel the uneven torque of reciprocating steam power—the periodic tugs—as the train returned to speed and again began to produce its soothing cover of sounds. The nagging of the porter's call buzzer was the next thing he heard, and it woke him to a room flooded with the yellow light of sunrise. "It's 6 o'clock, sir, Central Standard Time," the porter said. "We'll be in Elkhart in a few minutes."

Rudy slid open his door. With privacy protected by zipped curtains, he backed into the hall, released the catch on the bed, and pushed it up into the wall. Twenty minutes later—shaved, washed up, and cologned, with his thick, wavy black hair combed straight back—Rudy tied his tie, then walked up to the diner for an omelet with crisp bacon, washed down with coffee poured steaming from a silver pot. By 7:30 he was finished with breakfast and once again settled in the observation car, hoping to witness a bit of drama about which he'd often heard. Here, on the approach to Englewood, Ill., just a few miles from Chicago, the rival Pennsylvania Railroad's line curved in from the south, forming a side-by-side straightaway with the Central, many tracks wide and shining in the hazy morning light.

As the routes joined, suddenly there it was: the *Broadway Limited*, pounding along behind a streamlined K4 Pacific-type steam locomotive, its crown of coal smoke laying back low along the roofs of the Pullmans. The *Broadway*, close to on time, was coming on strong. With driving rods flailing, the Pennsy's Tuscan red Pacific inched up until it was neck-and-neck with the *Century*, as both engineers whipped their iron steeds. The race didn't end until the trains slowed for their station stops at Englewood, then made their separate ways into downtown Chicago, the *Broadway* to Union Station and the *Century* to La Salle Street Station.

Rudy wondered idly if, 60 years from then, with the millennium approaching, the railroad would rename its train the *21st Century Limited*. He'd just watched a race between two extraordinary streamliners that epitomized the combination of speed, service, and magnificent equipment that the railroads would muster in one last bid for preeminence in the passenger business. How could he have known that it would never get any better, that this edition of *20th Century Limited* and *Broadway Limited* represented the high-water-mark of American transportation in general and the passenger train in particular?

Rudy scurried back to his roomette, since arrival at Chicago's La Salle Street Station was little more than ten minutes away. The porter had already taken his suitcase to the vestibule for unloading, but he returned to give Rudy's dark suit a good brushing with his whisk broom. He took down the brown paper hat bag with the familiar Pullman logo in blue and exhumed Rudy's straw hat.

Within minutes the *Century* sighed to a stop. Rudy glanced at his pocket watch and wasn't surprised to see that it read 9 o'clock on the button. (He'd set it to Central Daylight Time.) He stepped off the *City of Toledo*, consigned his suitcase to a redcap, and headed toward the station concourse, past the dormitory-lounge and baggage-mail cars, now coated with a patina of road dust. He walked past the massive streamlined

Washed in low, late-afternoon sun and looking resplendent in its original dress, No. 25 steams north along the Hudson River on a June afternoon. This intricate color scheme, conceived by industrial designer Henry Dreyfuss, features black roofs and light gray flanks, dark gray pier panels between windows, with two broad aluminum stripes running through them. Narrow aluminum stripes run at the top and bottom of the sides, and blue stripes delineate the grays. Central began tinkering with this scheme almost immediately, and over the years the direction was always toward simplicity. ED NOWAK, NEW YORK CENTRAL, PETER V. TILP COLLECTION

LEFT: The *20th Century Limited* is brand new in June 1938 as it curves westbound into Peekskill, N.Y., a blue-collar Hudson River town. The luxurious *Island*-series observation car is generous with public space, offering both a solarium room in the rounded end and a lounge forward of that. Just ahead in the consist is an *Imperial*-series Pullman with four compartments, two drawing rooms, and four double bedrooms. Since the *Island* car carries only a master room (the train's premier accommodation) and a double bedroom, a good deal of deluxe space is located to the rear of the train. ED NOWAK, NEW YORK CENTRAL, PETER V. TILP COLLECTION

Hudson, loud with the roar of steam lifting pop valves—an exhilarating if monstrous presence.

Chicago! Here was the poet Sandburg's "player with railroads," the hub from which many of the country's finest passenger trains spoked. It was also the home of The Pullman Company, the greatest name in passenger railroading, and the place where George Mortimer Pullman set his great enterprise in motion. It had been a long haul from railroading's early days to the luxury of Pullman's first "Palace cars," let alone the exquisite pampering of the streamlined *20th Century Limited*—arguably the greatest train ever made.

2

THE EARLY YEARS

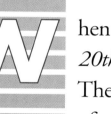**W**hen does the story of the *20th Century Limited* begin? The most obvious answer, of course, is June 15, 1902, when the train of that name was inaugurated. Other dates suggest themselves, however. The longest reach and farthest stretch would be August 1831 when a diminutive but ultimately unsuccessful steam locomotive named *De Witt Clinton* hauled a short train of small cars (clones of stagecoaches) over the tracks of the Mohawk & Hudson Rail Road. Connecting Schenectady, N.Y., with Albany, this pioneering 16-mile line was

The dawn of a *Century*. On this bright June morning in 1902, the twentieth century is (depending on how you count) less than a year and a half old—and its namesake train less than a day. Behind Atlantic No. 2960, this *20th Century Limited*—small but mighty in style, with a remarkably bright future—is caught here on its inaugural run . . . or so historians attempting to identify this picture have assumed. Just four cars long, the train is one short of the standard five of the early years. Probably even George H. Daniels, the Central's general passenger agent and godfather of the *Century*, would have had trouble that day imagining the long trains that would run in multiple sections 20 years hence. NEW YORK CENTRAL, PETER V. TILP COLLECTION

the oldest among the countless railways that would in time become the far-flung, heroic New York Central System, which by the end of the nineteenth century would embrace more than 10,000 route-miles in 11 states and two provinces.

A much more plausible date for the *Century*'s spark of creation is 1893, when the World's Columbian Exposition opened in Chicago, and railroads serving that city fielded new luxury trains for the travelers who flocked to that famous world's fair. New York Central's arch-rival, the Pennsylvania Railroad, inaugurated the *Pennsylvania Special*, while the Central added the *Exposition Flyer* on a 20-hour schedule that forecast the *Century*'s first timing nine years hence. Assuming that there wasn't enough non-fair-related business to sustain so fast and luxurious a service, the Central withdrew the *Flyer* when the Exposition ended that fall.

A date more plausible still is November 1897, when the *Lake Shore Limited* was inaugurated as NYC's first regularly scheduled super-luxury service. Running into Chicago on the Lake Shore & Michigan Southern Railway (as did the *Exposition Flyer*), the train took 24 hours to make the New York City–Chicago run, four more than the *Flyer* needed and the

Much is made of computer technology's ability to alter photographs, but the practice of visual deception started long before the electronic age. The black-and-white image BELOW captures a brand-new *20th Century* on the Lake Shore & Michigan Southern behind one of the railroad's elegant J40-class 2-6-2s, which stood tall on 79-inch drivers and were fleet of foot. The photo is obviously posed, the train static, basking in perfect lighting—no doubt a public-relations officer's set-up. Through the magic of darkroom trickery and early colorization, however, the photo serves as a basis for the postcard at LEFT. Now the scene has quite a different feel, romantic and moonlit, with the seemingly speeding train skirting Lake Erie—imported for the occasion. The card, which dates from the era when the post office reserved the entire back of cards for the address, was postmarked in 1906. BELOW, NEW YORK CENTRAL, PETER V. TILP COLLECTION; LEFT, WILLIAM F. HOWES JR. COLLECTION

20TH CENTURY LIMITED

COPYRIGHT, 1906, BY THE
LAKE SHORE & MICHIGAN SOUTHERN RAILWAY

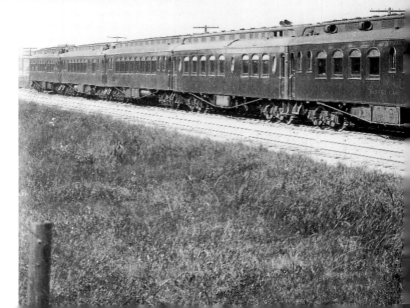

Century would need. The *Lake Shore Limited* was an elegant train indeed, the last great collaboration between New York Central and Buffalo-based Wagner Palace Car Company before this prestigious builder and operator of sleeping cars was swallowed up, like virtually all the others before it had been, by The Pullman Company (formerly the Pullman Palace Car Company) in 1899.

Wagner was long the sleeping-car company of choice for New York Central, and the railroad remained loyal to Wagner's end. Actually, founder Webster Wagner (who, in a grotesquely ironic twist, was killed in 1892 aboard one of his own cars in a head-on collision) had worked for the Central and had begun his sleeping-car operation with the backing of Commodore Cornelius Vanderbilt, the giant figure who looms over the New York Central's history. In fact, Wagner's company was founded as the New York Central Sleeping Car Company, which became a fierce rival of the octopus-like Pullman Palace Car Company.

Wagner cars had been used to equip the *Exposition Flyer*, and in fact Wagner and NYC had a joint exhibit at the Columbian Exposition. The *Lake Shore Limited*—which included a Boston section, joining or splitting from the New York City train at Albany—was as elegant as anything then-rival Pullman could offer. The all-first-class seven-car consists included a buffet-library-smoking car with baggage compartment, a parlor car, a diner, three sleepers, and an open-platform observation car containing a lounge, library, and eight compartment-staterooms. Riding on six-wheel trucks (wheel assemblies), these dark-liveried "composite" cars (wood, with iron reinforcing) were stylishly lined out. "*The Lake Shore Limited*" was inscribed on the letterboards at each car's ends. Here then was a worthy ancestor of the *20th Century Limited*, which lay only five years in the future.

Many famous names had a role in the *20th Century Limited* story. Cornelius Vanderbilt in effect created the railroad over which it ran.

George M. Pullman founded the company that equipped the train in all its versions and staffed and operated its sleepers for most of its life. Henry Dreyfuss designed its most stylish incarnation. Dwight Eisenhower officiated at the inauguration of its last, handsome re-equipping in 1948. Countless celebrities rode it, literally anyone who was anyone.

But the name most instrumental to the train, one that enjoyed some contemporary notoriety but is virtually forgotten today, is George Henry Daniels, who served as New York Central's general passenger agent throughout the 1890s and into the twentieth century. He is truly the father of the train that would carry the name of that new century—a name he selected for it.

Daniels, who appears in his portrait as rotund, white-haired, and clean-shaven but for a luxuriant goatee, accumulated a long list of claims to fame during his stint as general passenger agent, which lasted from 1889 to 1907. The earliest train to appear on that list was the *Empire State Express*. Inaugurated in October 1891 as a day service between New York City and Buffalo, it carried the cachet of speed throughout its career, having averaged over 60 miles per hour including stops, on a pre-inaugural test run between its endpoint cities. Daniels' next train of note was the *Exposition Flyer*, followed by the *Lake Shore Limited*.

A part of the Central's Columbian Exposition story along with the *Flyer* was an American-type locomotive numbered 999, a popular exhibit there. This gloriously high-drivered speedster was quintessentially elegant and astonishingly quick. (In truth, its 84-inch drivers turned out to be too tall to muster much pulling power; it was a greyhound, not a husky.) On May 10, 1893, with Charles Hogan's hand on the throttle and the consist of the *Empire State Express* trailing behind, No. 999 raced along the level, flat speedway between Batavia, N.Y., and Buffalo at an unprecedented 112 miles per hour. Needless to say, Daniels spread the word of this great feat far and wide, and he eventually persuaded the postmaster general to include an image of the 999 pulling the *Empire State Express* in the Pan American Exposition postage series. Issued in 1901, these five stamps also included pictures of a Great Lakes steamboat, an ocean liner, an automobile, the canal locks at Sault Ste. Marie, and the Niagara Falls suspension bridge.

Daniels took charge of the railroad's dining-car and lunchroom services and improved them. He coined the moniker "America's Greatest Railroad" for the Central. (Competitor Pennsylvania, on the other hand, called itself "The Standard Railroad of the World," an equally cheeky and no less accurate boast.) He created the publications *The Four-Track News* and *Health and Pleasure on America's Greatest Railroad*. Daniels was the man behind both the name and concept of the redcap. "Free attendant Service at Grand Central Station, N.Y. Ask the man with the RED CAP to carry your bag and show you to your cab, car, or elevated train," read an 1896 ad. "This service is free. The New York Central pays for it." Eventually, redcaps could be found in stations across the land.

But George H. Daniels' greatest and most memorable accomplishment was the *20th Century*

This inaugural brochure summarizes the equipment makeup (consists) and schedules. It carries, on the cover, two names of considerable importance to New York Central and the *20th Century Limited*. George H. Daniels was instrumental in shaping and then publicizing "The Greatest Train in the World." Alfred H. Smith would become president of the railroad, serving from 1914 to 1924, with a few years off to act as Eastern Regional Director of the United States Railroad Administration during World War I. PETER V. TILP COLLECTION

20 HOURS
BETWEEN
NEW YORK
AND
CHICAGO
BY
"THE **20**TH **CENTURY LIMITED**"
OF THE
NEW YORK CENTRAL
and **LAKE SHORE**
1902

A.H.SMITH
GENERAL SUPERINTENDENT

GEO. H. DANIELS
GENERAL PASSENGER AGENT

Limited, a perfect train with the perfect name. As the century turned, numerous pieces fell into place that allowed this dream train to become a reality. In the upper echelons of management, the guard was changing. In 1898, Chauncey Depew retired as president of the New York Central and replaced Cornelius Vanderbilt (who was in ill health and would die the following year) as chairman of the board. After a brief stint by Samuel Callaway, William H. Newman took over as president in 1901, ushering in a period of substantial upgrading for the Central. Under the direction of General William J. Wilgus, the railroad's chief engineer, right-of-way improvements went forward. Curves were eased and grades moderated. Heavier ballast was laid, along with the country's first 100-pound, six-inch-high rail. Signaling was improved. With infrastructure in place, all that remained was for a train worthy of it to be created, named, and promoted. Daniels was just the man to accomplish these latter two tasks.

The *20th Century Limited* would revert to the 20-hour timings of the *Exposition Flyer*, bettering by four hours the then-current carding of the *Lake Shore Limited*. "The *20th Century Limited*, every day of the year, between New York and Chicago via New York Central and Lake Shore, 980 miles in 20 hours," read a pre-inaugural advertisement. "Fastest long distance train in the world, will be placed in service June 15, 1902."

Especially by the multi-section standards that would prevail a few decades hence, the initial consists of the *Century* were modest in length and capacity (if not in amenities)—just five cars, accommodating a mere 42 passengers. (Throughout its career, because of the train's speed, only

"The 20th Century Limited."

A NEW 20-HOUR TRAIN

Between New York and Chicago
By the New York Central and Lake Shore.

MILES.		DAILY.
0	Lv. New York..............	2.45 P. M.
143	Ar. Albany	5.35 P. M.
143	Lv. Albany	5.39 P. M.
238	Lv. Utica.................	7.34 P. M.
291	Ar. Syracuse	8.38 P. M.
291	Lv. Syracuse	8.42 P. M.
376	Lv. Rochester............10.15	P. M.
440	Ar. Buffalo (East. Time)..11.45	P. M.
440	Lv. Buffalo (Cent. Time)..10.50	P. M.
623	Ar. Cleveland............	2.27 A. M.
736	Ar. Toledo	4.45 A. M.
879	Ar. Elkhart..............	7.27 A. M.
980	Ar. Chicago..............	9.45 A. M.

NEW PULLMAN EQUIPMENT.

A combined baggage, buffet, smoking and library car.

Two twelve-section, drawing-room and state-room sleeping-cars.

A private compartment (eight state-rooms) sleeping and observation car.

A dining-car serving all meals.

"The 20th Century Limited."

A NEW 20-HOUR TRAIN

Between Chicago and New York
By the Lake Shore and New York Central.

MILES.		DAILY.
0	Lv. Chicago 12.30	NOON
101	Lv. Elkhart..............	2.43 P. M.
244	Lv. Toledo	5.25 P. M.
357	Lv. Cleveland...........	7.43 P. M.
452	Lv. Erie.................	9.40 P. M.
540	Ar. Buffalo (Cent. Time)..11.30	P. M.
540	Lv. Buffalo (East. Time)..12.34	A. M.
609	Ar. Rochester...........	1.56 A. M.
689	Ar. Syracuse	3.29 A. M.
742	Ar. Utica.................	4.34 A. M.
837	Ar. Albany	6.32 A. M.
837	Lv. Albany	6.35 A. M.
980	Ar. New York	9.30 A. M.

IT SAVES A DAY.

The new 20-hour train of the New York Central and Lake Shore enables a man to do a day's work in New York and be in Chicago next morning.

980 MILES IN 20 HOURS.

The new " 20th Century Limited" of the New York Central and Lake Shore will do this every day, and effect a great saving to the busy man who travels between the East and West.

The *20th Century Limited* has grown considerably from its first years by the time it is captured here, running eastbound behind a Pacific near Peekskill, N.Y., with the Hudson River in the background. The all-Pullman consist is substantial but still leads off with a combine, which contains the train's rolling "men's club"—the lounge where cigar smoke could be expected to hang heavy in the air. E. L. DE GOLYER JR. PHOTOGRAPH COLLECTION, SOUTHERN METHODIST UNIVERSITY, DALLAS, TEXAS; ITEM COLLECTION NO. AG1982.232

two consists, or trainsets, were required to protect the *Century's* schedule.) Those five cars, plus a locomotive to haul them, cost just $115,000. In fact, the Central's total investment in its first *20th Century Limited*—15 sleeping cars, four club cars, two diners, and seven locomotives—totaled a modest $525,000. Later costs for the train would dwarf these numbers.

The train was traditional in configuration and equipment. In fact, for the first year and more, it operated with cars that had been built by Wagner and Pullman for the *Lake Shore Limited* and other predecessor trains. Though hand-me-downs, with train names on the cars' Pullman-green flanks painted over and re-stenciled, these vehicles were no slouches. Gems of the consist, carrying the marker lights, were Wagner-built (and refurbished by Pullman after the 1899 takeover) observation-compartment-lounge cars *Alroy* and *Sappho*. Up front were baggage-buffet-smoking-library "combine" cars *Decius* and *Cyrus*. These smoke-filled cars at the head of the consist were male bastions, a tradition that lasted even into the streamline era. On the other hand, the open-platform observations at the rear were the province of the women and non-smoking males. Rounding out the consists were pairs of 12-section 1-drawing room 1-stateroom sleepers (*Petruchio*, *Philario*, *Gonzalo*, and *Benvolio*) and the dining cars.

Packed into these cars were many of the amenities for which the train would become so famous: barber shop, valet, maid, stenographer. (The provision of these particular services made it very clear just what clientele the Central expected to attract with its new train: the moneyed, used to being attended, and successful men of commerce who might

need to dash off a letter on the spur of the moment.) The cars were opulent and elegant, with oval windows of stained glass. The train's electric lights glowed with power from axle generators—an innovation at the time, with the *Century* among the first trains to embrace it. The *Lake Shore Limited*, on the other hand, carried a dynamo in its baggage car to generate the power needed to illuminate its cars. (Axle generators would become a staple of passenger railroading that lasted some six decades, until diesel engines within locomotives began being used to generate "head-end power" for lights, heat, and air conditioning.)

"A marvelous service between New York and Chicago" is what a modest black-and-white brochure (printed on July 17, 1902, by American Bank Note Co.) said about the train. The flyer, published under the amalgamation of the New York Central & Hudson River Railroad and the Lake Shore & Michigan Southern, the two components of New York Central Lines that operated the *Century*, listed stops at Albany, Utica, Syracuse, Rochester, Buffalo, Cleveland, Toledo, and Elkhart. Then the little folder summarized: "One 20-hour train, four 24-hour trains and three slower trains every day" between New York and Chicago. After enumerating trains to Niagara Falls, Montreal, and Boston, it ended with an uncharacteristically modest claim: "An adequate service by the New York Central Lines."

Original timings for the *Century* (a train to which the adjective "adequate" was never applied) called for a westbound departure from New York's Grand Central Station at 2:45 P.M. with arrival at Chicago's La Salle Street Station at 9:45 A.M. Eastbound departure was at 12:30 P.M.

(the earlier time reflecting the loss of an hour in moving from Central to Eastern time, as opposed to the gain westbound), with arrival at 9:30 A.M.

Certain anecdotes about the *Century's* initial run have become almost mythic, recounted by all the noted chroniclers of the train, including Lucius Beebe, Arthur Dubin, and Alvin Harlow in his *The Road of the Century.* One is the remarks of a British journalist, who felt that the train's aspirations as to speed were impossibly high.

"Surely it is only an experiment," he wrote—and a silver anniversary booklet for the *Century* cited, and those historians have subsequently quoted. "There are over 900 miles between the two American cities. Can so high a rate of speed as will be necessary to accomplish the feat be maintained daily without injury to the engine, the rails and the coaches? The operators will soon find that they are wasting fortunes in keeping their property in condition, and then, loving money better than notoriety, the twenty-hour project will be abandoned."

Prescient he wasn't, that Brit, since in the course of its entire 65-year career the *20th Century Limited* never needed more than a carded 20 hours to make the run between New York and Chicago. In fact, for most of its history it required less time to make the trip. In 1905, for instance, the schedule was cut to a remarkable 18 hours. Central executives were sanguine about speed at the time of the train's inauguration, and why

not? In 1893, the railroad had run the *Exposition Flyer* on what would be the timings for the new *Century*. Two years later, in 1895, a test train had streaked from Chicago to Buffalo, a distance of 525 miles, at an average speed of 65 miles per hour.

Initial motive power for the *Century* on the New York Central & Hudson River were Atlantic-type 4-4-2 ("4-4-2" translating as four pilot wheels, four driving wheels, two trailing wheels) steam locomotives numbered in the 2900-series. On the Lake Shore & Michigan Southern portion of the run, handsome J40-class Prairie types (2-6-2s), high-drivered locomotives built by Brooks Locomotives Works, at first did the honors. In 1904 they were supplanted by I1-class Ten-Wheelers (4-6-0s) from the same builder, and by the end of the decade Class K2 Pacifics (4-6-2s) were in charge. The cars evolved quickly too. By 1904 the *Century* had been completely re-equipped with cars built especially for that train—by The Pullman Company, of course.

On the first trip westbound trip out of Grand Central Station, motive power was Atlantic No. 2960. In the Pullmans trailing behind were just 27 passengers, including (and this is another oft-quoted anecdote) John W. "Bet-a-Million" Gates, an infamous high roller at the turn of the century who had made his money selling barbed wire to a westering nation. Arriving at Chicago, he raved about the *Century*'s speed and told the press that the new train would make New York City a suburb of Chicago. So pleased with the experience was he that Gates hopped back on the train and returned to New York City—where he told the press there that Chicago would now be a suburb of New York.

In any event, from the beginning, the *Century* caught the public's fancy for its speed, luxury, and prestige, as well as for the wealth, social status, and celebrity of its passengers. Another asset promoted from the outset was its route. "The topography of the country through which a train is operated is always of vital importance to the Operating Department of a railroad," boasted the silver anniversary booklet a quarter century later. "In this respect the New York Central is indeed fortunate in its Water Level Route. A study of a map of the eastern States shows that the main line of the New York Central follows a water level route laid out by Nature's engineers and the only water level route between New York and the Mississippi Valley."

Rolling out of Grand Central Station, passengers aboard those first runs of the *Century* (as indeed *Century* passengers would do for 65 years to come) followed the Harlem River north for a few miles to Spuyten Duyvil, where it joined the Hudson. For the next 131 miles to Albany, the tracks would shadow the Hudson River—about as grade-free a route as you can find, since the Hudson is tidal all that way. The scenery here was splendid, and that June day when the train began was among the year's longest. This was fortunate, since—so fast was the *Century*'s timing—most of its run would always be made after dark. First came the dramatically sheer cliffs of the Palisades, across the river in New Jersey. The mountainous "Highlands of the Hudson," a region often compared to Germany's Rhine Valley, followed shortly.

Not far beyond Albany (though a steep West Albany Hill did stand in the way, presenting the route's greatest operating challenge), the tracks regained water, paralleling the Mohawk River all the way to Syracuse, where the line entered the Lake Ontario watershed. Shortly before midnight, just west of Buffalo, No. 25, the westbound *Century*, would pass No. 26, its eastbound counterpart. From Buffalo through Cleveland to Toledo, a distance of 290 miles, Central rails ran along Lake Erie's southern shore, then—after slipping across the rolling prairies of Indiana—headed into Chicago by skirting the waters of Lake Michigan.

If the route was splendid, far outshining that of the Central's nemesis, the Pennsylvania Railroad, in operating ease, its eastern portal was

Five of six semaphores show "clear" at Riverdale, N.Y., as the westbound *Century* rolls north along the Hudson River in 1914 behind a T-motor, still well within the electrified New York City commutation district. The photo appears to have been taken from the back of a train that has caused the fifth semaphore from the left to drop to the horizontal "stop" position. Within seconds the far-left blade will also drop to horizontal, indicating that the *Century* is occupying the block ahead and prohibiting another train from entering it. The two non-electrified tracks at right lead to Central's West Side Freight Line, which brought produce and other goods into Manhattan. The four-track, third-rail-equipped main line runs all the way from Grand Central to Harmon.

splendid, too. And once again Central one-upped the Pennsy, which at that time still terminated its trains on the west bank of the Hudson, in New Jersey. Central, on the other hand, had in its Grand Central Station a station that was both grand and central—in Midtown Manhattan, New York City's up-and-coming heart. On the corner of Fourth (now Lexington) Avenue and 42nd Street, Grand Central Depot had opened in October 1871. Used by the New York Central & Hudson River Railroad and New York & Harlem Railroad (both of which became part of the New

By the time this photograph of Grand Central Station was made, the turn-of-the-century expansion had been completed, with three stories added for offices. The facade is completely new, in the French Renaissance style, and domed towers have replaced the mansard-roofed ones of predecessor Grand Central Depot. This view looks down 42nd Street, with its streetcars and modest pedestrian bustle. Vanderbilt Avenue runs into 42nd Street in the center of the photo.
NEW YORK CENTRAL

York Central System) and the New York & New Haven Railroad, this 12-track station was imposing, with five towers. Then, in 1900, just two years before the *Century's* inaugural, it was dramatically expanded and modified (and renamed Grand Central Station), receiving an additional three stories of offices; by this time traffic had increased threefold over 1871 levels. Tracks were expanded to 19, served by 11 platforms. A single waiting room replaced the three smaller ones (each used by a single railroad) that previously existed. William J. Wilgus, the New York Central & Hudson River's chief engineer (who would be responsible for the brilliant concepts behind the Grand Central Terminal that would open in the same space in 1913) was instrumental in making practical improvements.

In due course the *20th Century Limited's* departures from Grand Central would acquire that ultimate element of cachet—the red carpet, a glamorous welcome to passengers boarding the cars of what New York Central dubbed "The Greatest Train in the World." Legend has it that this famous carpet (which didn't appear at Chicago's La Salle Street station until decades later, after World War II) was another inspiration of endlessly creative General Passenger Agent George Daniels. Daniels, it's said, noticed that, at the Vanderbilts' Fifth Avenue mansion in New York, a footman would lay down a red carpet for family members to tread between carriage and house. "Why not do that for our passengers?" he thought. Thus one of the train's most hallowed traditions was born.

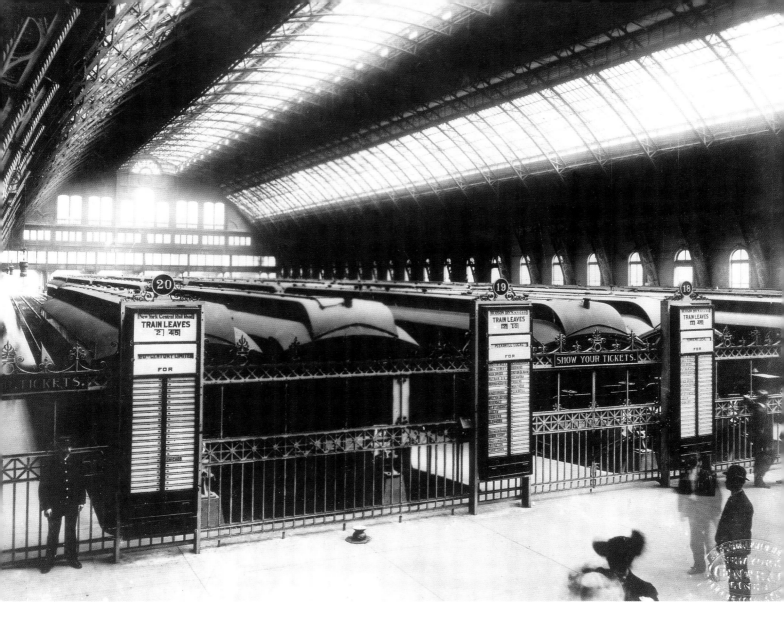

It's 1902, the year of the *20th Century Limited*'s inaugural, and the gate sign for track 20 is marked up for that train. Though the departure time—2:45—is posted, the destinations are not—nor is the train in place, just a single car. Passengers are commanded by signs above the gates to "Show your tickets" before boarding. The grillwork fencing the platforms from the concourse was added in the 1900 remodeling, while the vast, airy trainshed itself predates it.
NEW YORK CENTRAL

What was good for New York would be good for Boston, New York Central executives felt, so in 1909 a Boston section of the *Century* was inaugurated over the Boston & Albany, another New York Central Lines affiliate. Amenities were no fewer than aboard the main New York City section, with which the Boston train was joined (or from which severed, eastbound) at Albany. Running times were some two hours longer, however, because of substantial grades through the Berkshire Mountains. This, in fact, was decidedly *not* a water level route.

The passenger traffic department of the NYC&HR and LS&MS issued a Joint Manual of Instructions for the Central's premier trains: Nos. 25 and 26, the *20th Century Limited*, and Nos. 19 and 22, the *Lake Shore Limited*. Addressed to "ticket agents, conductors and others interested," it opened this way:

"It is the desire and intention of the Management of the New York Central Lines that the service afforded by its limited trains shall be as nearly perfect as it is possible to make it. The higher fares charged and the superior accommodations furnished," the 1908 booklet continued, "naturally attract passengers who expect, and have the right to expect, every attention."

Right from the beginning, the reality aboard the *20th Century Limited* met those high expectations. Passengers did indeed receive "every attention."

39

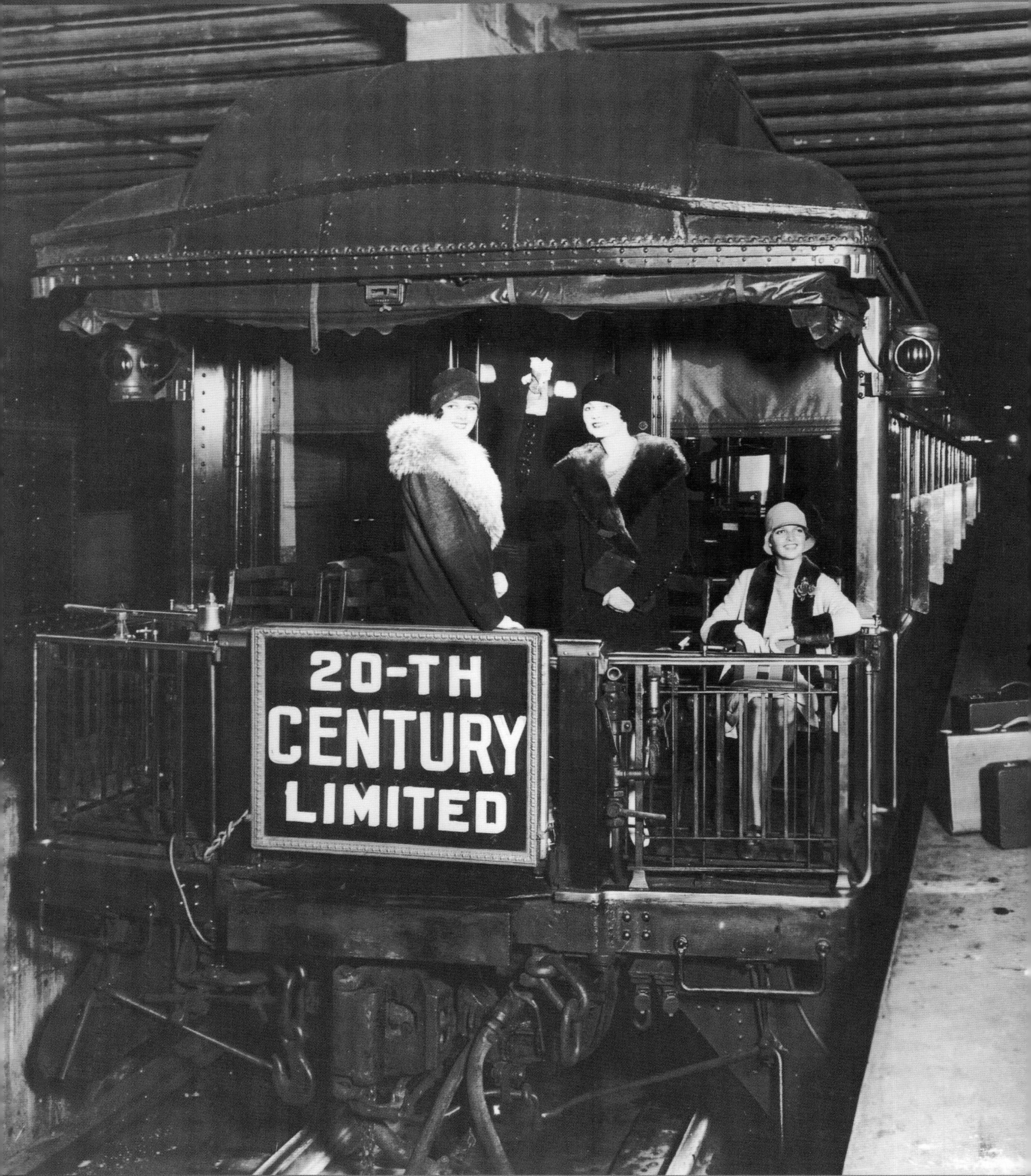
20-TH
CENTURY
LIMITED

3

ABUNDANT CENTURYS: THE HEAVYWEIGHT YEARS

No doubt there's a certain irony in this: The era that brought the *20th Century Limited* its greatest glory had as its most significant catalyst New York Central's most noted rival, the Pennsylvania Railroad. For it was in the 1920s, deep in the railroading period that has come to be called the "heavyweight era," when passenger cars were substantial battleships built of riveted steel, that the *Century* achieved its apex in terms of fame and frequency. (The designation "heavyweight" is a product of the much-later "streamline" or "lightweight" era,

Beautiful, stylish women often rode the *20th Century Limited,* but this view from April 1931 is of models showing the latest fashions. The platform awning is strapped up, providing no distraction. The redcap deals with the women's luggage, including a hatbox. Dimly visible to the left is another section of the *Century.* NEW YORK CENTRAL

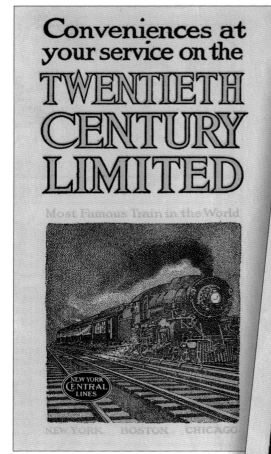

when the term was coined to distinguish the old cars from the new.)

Iron and steel passenger cars were slow in coming, though the mode had demonstrable and recognizable benefits virtually from the beginning of railroading. Throughout the latter half of the nineteenth century, dozens of prototypes for metal cars were projected and a handful built as demonstrators—none of which caught on. In fact, a few iron cars actually predated 1850. Bernard Joachim La Mothe, a New York City physician, was among their most persistent proponents, with nine patents and four cars actually built. Even John A. Roebling, builder of the Brooklyn Bridge and among the era's most noted engineers, half-heartedly turned his attention to the concept.

This saga, carefully detailed by William H. White Jr. in his definitive book *The American Railroad Passenger Car*, had everything to do with money. Metal cars would be significantly more costly to build and, since they would be much heavier, more costly to haul. Their most obvious virtue was safety in the event of a catastrophic accident. The railroads did not find this a highly marketable feature, since they were not eager to acknowledge the probability of such a mishap. So railroad executives held back, in spite of the predictable clamoring in the press every time a significant train accident occurred and passengers died. (Steel freight cars, with their increased carrying capacity, were more enthusiastically embraced by the industry than steel passenger cars, which offered only a safer ride.)

Though La Mothe's efforts ultimately came to naught, when the steel-car breakthrough finally happened it was in his hometown, and it

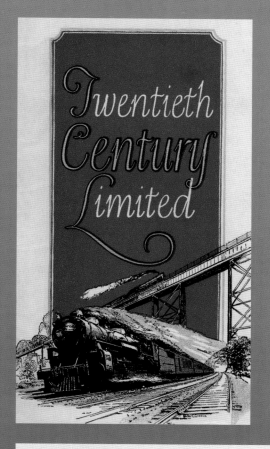

WESTBOUND				EASTBOUND		
		No. 25—Daily				No. 26—Daily
	N.Y.C.R.R.	PM			N.Y.C.R.R	PM
Lv.	New York (G.C. Term.) (E.T.)	2:45		*Lv*	Chicago (LaSalle St Sta.)(C.T.)	12:40
Lv.	Harmon	h3:38		*Lv.*	Englewood	12:53
	B. & A. R.R			*Ar.*	Albany	e6:27
Lv.	Boston (South Station)	12:30			B. & A. R.R.	
Lv	Worcester	1:37		*Ar*	Pittsfield	8:07
Lv	Springfield	2:55		*Ar*	Springfield	9:32
Lv	Pittsfield	4:30		*Ar*	Worcester	10:55
Lv.	Albany	h5:49		*Ar*	Boston (South Station)	12.00
Lv.	Utica	h7:43				
Lv.	Syracuse	h8:53		*Ar*	Harmon	i8:46
Lv.	Rochester	h10:25		*Ar*	New York (G. C. Term) (E.T.)	9:40
Ar.	Elkhart (C. T.)	7:21				AM
Ar.	Englewood	9:30				
Ar.	Chicago (La Salle St. Sta.)(C.T.)	9:45				
		AM				

e Stops to discharge Chicago passengers only.   i Stops only to discharge passengers.   h Stops to receive passengers only.
E.T.—*Eastern Time*—Toledo and East   C.T.—*Central Time*—West of Toledo

THE WATER LEVEL ROUTE   YOU CAN SLEEP

Club Car ~

Stock Market Quotations—Posted in Club Car en route.

Newspapers, Etc.—Illustrated weeklies, newspapers and Official Railway Guide provided for use of patrons.

Mail Box—In Club Car. Letters stamped and deposited therein will be posted at earliest opportunity to insure prompt delivery. Letters may also be handed to the stenographer for posting.

Sporting Events—The results of baseball games, American and National League, principal football games and other important sporting events are posted in the Club Car.

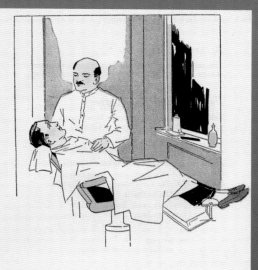

Barber & Valet ~

IN CLUB CAR

Barber—Prices for Men: Shave 30c., haircut 75c., shampoo 50c., massage 50c., trimming beard 35c., singeing 25c., tonic 25c., Prices for ladies :Shingle bob $1.00, straight bob 75c., trimming hair 75c., shampoo 75c., facial massage 75c.

Valet—Clothing sponged and pressed over night. Suits $1.50, overcoats $1.00, coat 75c., trousers 50c., vest 25c., skirts 75c.

Shower Bath—Barber will make all arrangements. Charge 50c.

THE WATER LEVEL ROUTE   YOU CAN SLEEP

This 1926 brochure recaps the special features of the *Century* in the pre-Hudson heavyweight era. The cover sketch shows a K3 Pacific roaring south along the Hudson River with No. 26 passing under the bridge of the Castleton Cutoff, which carries freight traffic off the Boston & Albany over the Hudson and the Central's Albany–New York main and into Selkirk Yard, west of the river. An interesting tidbit inside recounts the staffing. At any given time the crew aboard a *Century* section of typical length numbered 32: one engineer, one fireman, one railroad conductor, one Pullman conductor, one baggageman, two brakemen, ten porters, one maid, one barber, one stenographer, one steward, four cooks, and seven waiters. The engineer and fireman changed eight times between New York and Chicago and the railroad conductor, brakemen, and baggageman three times. PETER V. TILP COLLECTION

occurred underground, with the Pennsylvania Railroad being the key player, at least among mainline carriers. In 1901 the Interborough Rapid Transit, New York's first subway, was being built, and safety in the tunnels was an issue. With this in mind, the IRT retained George Gibbs—a noted engineer who would later achieve even greater recognition with the PRR—to consult on car design. Though Gibbs recommended all-steel cars, the IRT initially went with copper-sheathed wood cars that had steel frames. However, a calamitous collision and fire in the Paris subway changed management's mind, and in 1904 IRT ordered 200 all-steel cars from American Car & Foundry.

This, along with an order for 134 similar cars by commuter-carrying Long Island Rail Road, a PRR subsidiary, began the production era of all-steel passenger cars. LIRR's requisition was precipitated by its plans to enter Manhattan and the new Pennsylvania Station through the East River Tunnels. PRR would then have access to Sunnyside Yards—the future service and storage facility for the road's passenger trains—and a through route to New England via the Hell Gate Bridge. Construction of the East River and Hudson River tunnels would extend the PRR main line from

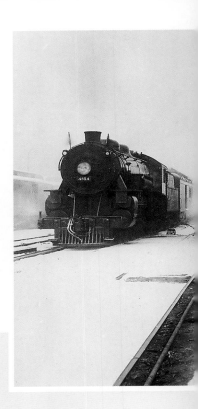

New Jersey to the heart of Manhattan, an advantage of access held solely by the New York Central until then. This development was at the heart of PRR's monumental upgrading and preceded its most visible component, the magnificent Pennsylvania Station, opening in 1910.

A. J. Cassatt, president of the Pennsylvania at this time of expansion, felt from the beginning that PRR must have fireproof, all-steel cars for its tunnels. To this end, Cassatt offered the railroad's car shops at Altoona, Pa., for building the first, experimental steel car for the IRT in 1903, the same year digging began on the PRR tunnels. The Altoona Shops fabricated an experimental coach for "steam-road" (as opposed to rapid-transit, trolley, or interurban) service three years later. In 1907 PRR placed its first order for all-steel P-70-class day coaches, which would in time make up one of the most extensive and famous passenger-car fleets ever built. PRR estimated that it would need 1,000 coaches, diners, and baggage cars plus 500 Pullman sleepers and parlor cars when Penn Station opened. By 1912, in point of fact, PRR had some 2,800 heavyweight cars in service system-wide. And on the West Coast, the Harriman Lines were buying substantial numbers of these all-steel cars as well.

Obviously, the New York Central, which proclaimed itself "America's Greatest Railroad," couldn't hold back in making this transition—especially for its preeminent *20th Century Limited*, "The Greatest Train in the World." Beginning in 1910, then, all-steel cars began arriving from The Pullman Company for the Central's flagship. Like the steel cars built for other railroads, they did not differ radically in design or construction from the wood or steel-framed composite cars that were their predecessors. The Pullman Company, in fact, was a conservative force in the wood-to-steel transition. No doubt the last thing the company wanted was for its vast fleet of wooden cars to become obsolete.

The new steel cars looked much like their predecessors both inside and out. In fact, some, including the *Century's* baggage-buffet cars of 1910, had their steel exterior walls grooved to look like wood—allegedly to quell fears of electrocution among nervous travelers in thunderstorms. Railroading typically has been an industry slow to embrace change, and the

continued on page 48

On a snowy, misty December day in 1924, five K3 Pacifics wait to charge east from Chicago's La Salle Street Station with a multiplicity of sections that was unusual even for the *Century*. Typically, only one section would make all stops, with intermediate passengers assigned to its cars. That section also carried the Railway Post Office car. Since they might well run early, the first sections of the *Century* would technically operate as multiple sections of the last-departing train, rather than as sections of No. 25 and 26, which would have required them to wait for carded time at each station stop. The K3s were a large and successful locomotive class; 281 were built between 1911 and 1925. NEW YORK CENTRAL, PETER V. TILP COLLECTION

45

This is a remarkable photographic record of the roll-by of a complete *20th Century Limited* from the mid 1920s, from locomotive to observation car. The engine is K3 Pacific No. 4907, notable in that the *Century*'s numbers, 25-26, are painted on the coal bunker of its tender. Baggage-buffet lounge-smoker *Delta*, built in September 1924, is the newest car in the consist; barber and stenographer would be found there. *Dana, Holland, Hardwick,* and (right behind the diner) *Winter* are 12-section 1-compartment 1-drawing room sleepers, built in 1921 or 1923. Just ahead of the dining car is 12-section 1-drawing room *St. Delphine* from 1924. The oldest car in the train by far is *Waldameer*, an 8-compartment lounge-observation that dates from 1911. Right ahead of it is 6-compartment 3-drawing room *Southey*. PETER V. TILP COLLECTION

46

WESTWARD BOUND,
IN THE MOHAWK VALLEY
The Twentieth Century Limited
NEW YORK CENTRAL LINES

Walter L. Greene

"Hudson along the Mohawk" could have been an alternate title for this painting by Walter L. Greene depicting the New York Central's most famous locomotive and train running along its second most famous river. Used for the railroad's 1929 calendar, this image shows J1a No. 5200, the "class engine" (because it was the first built of this engine class of locomotives and had the lowest number) streaking westward in the last yellow-pink light of evening. Number 5200 is carrying the green flags on its smokebox that tell railroaders along the route that there is a "second section following." Green flags or marker lights are a detail that Greene—and William Harnden Foster, who painted calendars for the railroad from 1922 to 1924, when Greene took over—invariably included in their paintings. Greene's last Central calendar was published in 1931, after which no calendars were painted until 1942, when Leslie Ragan became the calendar artist of choice. BILL STRASSNER COLLECTION

shift to all-steel cars was a gradual and somewhat grudging one.

Virtually every imaginable amenity possible on a passenger train had been accorded *Century* passengers in the flagship's first eight years, so little was left to add in the steel-car era—except the inherent benefit of greater safety. It might seem ironic, then, that the worst wreck of the *Century's* career took place early in the heavyweight years, on March 16, 1916, at Amherst, Ohio. In dense fog, the second section of a Chicago–Pittsburgh overnight train slammed into the first, strewing wreckage onto the westbound track—into which a late-running *20th Century Limited* then plowed. The death toll was 26 on the two Pittsburgh trains, but none of the *Century's* passengers or crew were even injured, so no irony.

The wreck producing the most casualties aboard the *Century* itself happened back in the wooden-car era, and at a most inopportune time—June 21, 1905, just a few days after the train's original 20-hour timing was dropped to 18. Though this derailment, which occurred at Mentor (also in Ohio) and killed 14 passengers and five crew members, was caused by a misaligned switch and not speed, it left the railroad open to criticism for its schedule acceleration. Ultimately, the safety record of the *20th Century Limited* supported the assumption that steel cars were safer.

Over the decades, the more things changed aboard the *Century*, the more they remained the same. The heavyweight trains continued the sterling service of their wooden-car predecessors, which the streamliners would continue in turn after 1938. The heavyweight era marched on through the teens and into the twenties as World War I came and went, and as the nation prospered so did the *20th Century Limited*. The number of *Century*s grew as more extra sections of the train were routinely operated. Green flags and marker lights atop the locomotives' smokeboxes—the industry-wide convention that advised other train crews and station and tower operators along the route that a second section was following—proliferated, though in the case of the *Century* they as often as not indicated a third, or fourth, or fifth section. As Mae West reportedly once said, "Too much of a good thing can be wonderful."

The late 1920s were a time of heady exuberance in the United States, and arguably the high-watermark for the *20th Century Limited*—and

IT PAYS TO RIDE THE CENTURY

GENTLEMEN:

This Train is your Office or your Club

YOU will find within the comfortable and spacious cars of the 20th Century Limited unique facilities for either work or relaxation. Hushed against the sound of travel—you breathe clean, fresh air in your air-conditioned, window-sealed quarters. If there is work to catch up on, the Century secretary is at your service. As are the barber, valet and the carefully selected porters.

Dinner tonight and breakfast tomorrow, skilfully prepared by the Century chef, will delight your palate. Retire, late or early, for a *real* night's sleep, unmindful that you are actually speeding onward. Rapidly you travel—but this world-famed Route is doubly guarded by the most efficient automatic safety system in the world.

At precisely 9 A.M. tomorrow, gentlemen, your trip will be complete—you will step from the Century, a full business day before you—feeling fresh and fit; and with a new conception of easy-going, comfortable travel. *It pays to ride the Century.*

New York to Chicago in 16½ Hours

Leave New York	5:30 P. M.
Leave Boston	3:00 P. M.
Arrive Chicago	9:00 A. M.
Leave Chicago	3:30 P. M.
Arrive New York	9:00 A. M.
Arrive Boston	11:10 A. M.

NEW YORK CENTRAL SYSTEM

The Water Level Route . . . You Can Sleep

This elegant little card, found in the accommodations aboard the *Century*, outlines the services that the train secretary might perform for the pampered passenger. Amenities like these made the *20th Century Limited* peer in service and style to the great ocean liners of the era such as the *Ile de France* and *Aquitania*. PETER V. TILP COLLECTION

THE TWENTIETH CENTURY LIMITED.
The train secretary will upon request, register your name in case a telegram may be received for you . . . write letters or telegrams that you may wish to send . . . make reservations of Pullman space beyond Chicago or New York, or reservations for return trip . . . arrange for transfer of hand baggage from train to residence, hotel or elsewhere, in Chicago or New York. Also wire for hotel reservations in any city or seats for theatrical attractions in New York or Chicago at regular telegraph tolls. The services of the Secretary are free.

This centerfold from a Central timetable underlines an important element of the train's character and status—its air of clubbiness and exclusivity. The railroad liked to promote its flagship as the domain of the rich and famous, especially the successful and moneyed businessman. The two gentlemen with boutonnieres certainly seem to be that. Standing on the open observation platform, they're enjoying what, for *Century* passengers at least, is on borrowed time, for streamlining is coming and with it round-end, enclosed observation cars. BILL STRASSNER COLLECTION

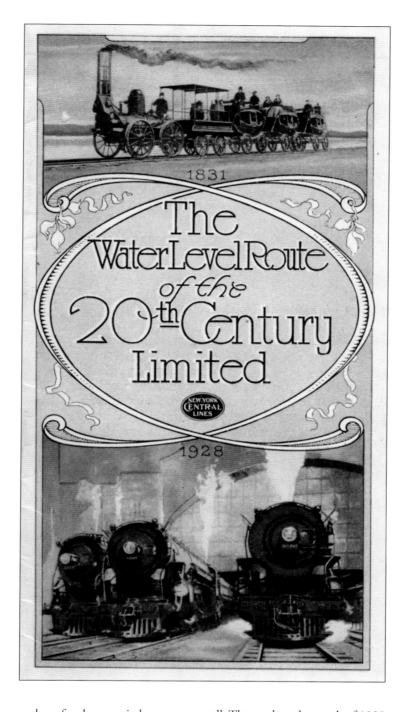

The Water Level Route of the 20th Century Limited

NEW YORK CENTRAL LINES

1831

1928

By 1928, J1 Hudsons have taken over from K3 Pacifics as the standard power for the *Century*. Here, in a painting by Walter L. Greene titled "Thoroughbreds" that appears on a 1928 brochure, three of them loom purposefully against the train shed of La Salle Street Station in Chicago, ready to lead No. 26 east in the multiple sections that were the era's norm. The locomotive on the right is J1a No. 5200, the prototype. The others are J1b's, the first production Hudsons. Passenger railroading had come a long way in the 97 years since the *De Witt Clinton* (illustrated at the top of the brochure) chugged 16 miles over the primitive track of the Mohawk & Hudson between Albany and Schenectady. KARL ZIMMERMANN COLLECTION

perhaps for the twentieth century as well. The stockmarket crash of 1929 and the Great Depression that followed were still unlooked-for, even unthinkable. Prohibition only fueled the party atmosphere and speakeasy culture, giving alcohol the added allure of the forbidden. In 1927 Charles Lindbergh made his stirring solo flight across the Atlantic and captivated America. Babe Ruth hit 60 home runs, a record that would stand for more than three decades. "Show Boat," the first great American musical, opened on Broadway.

Though perhaps Lindbergh and his *Spirit of St. Louis* (a name the Pennsylvania Railroad would later appropriate for one of its trains) might have been seen as a harbinger by a few of the most intuitive observers, for most Americans the difficulty and hardship of his transatlantic flight no doubt just underlined by contrast the comfort and safety routinely available on the rails of America. For this was the heyday of the American passenger train, with travel fueled by fortunes that were still growing. If

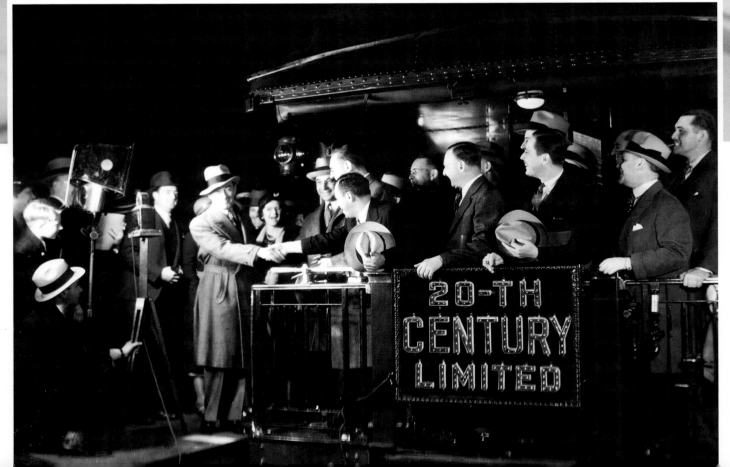

you could afford it, and in 1927 and 1928 many more could than ever before, rail was unquestionably the travel mode of choice, especially travel by Pullman.

Lindbergh and his barnstorming cronies notwithstanding, this was still the Railroad Age—though the highway and automotive lobbies had already wormed their way into positions of influence. At passenger railroading's peak, the country boasted some 140,000 railway stations, and 95 percent of the population lived near one of them. By the late 1920s, however, these numbers were about to change dramatically. The Depression, the automobile, and the commercial airliner would see to that. But for the moment the passenger train was riding high, and none higher than the *20th Century Limited*, the darling of the wealthy, famous, and stylish.

At the end of the Roaring Twenties, the Jazz Age so evocatively chronicled by F. Scott Fitzgerald, the *Century* was a *nonpareil.* "The schedule of the *Century* in both directions provides a daylight trip along the Hudson," advises an on-board brochure of the time. "Lap robes for use on the observation platform may be obtained from the porter in the observation car." And those who preferred to enjoy Hudson River vistas from their drawing rooms or compartments would never be disappointed, since all the *Century's* private rooms unfailingly faced the river while the aisle side of the cars faced the bluffs. Accomplishing this took considerable effort. At the storage and servicing yards—Mott Haven in New York and Root Street in Chicago—the club car at the head end and the open-platform observation car at the rear obviously had to be turned on a wye track to get them properly faced for their return journey. So did the diner, since it would never do to have the galley ahead of the dining area, possibly allowing cooking odors to blow back and take the appetites of the patrons. So the train was split up, the diner and lounges turned and the Pullmans not, then reassembled—a time-consuming process, but well worth it to make a trip on the *Century* as perfect as possible.

As well as a porter with lap robes, the observation car featured a stenographer, whose services were free. Along with taking dictation, he could help with telegrams (including wiring for Pullman reservations for the return trip). Western Union had messengers at the ready not only at Grand Central in New York, South Station in Boston, and La Salle Street in Chicago but at all intermediate station stops as well. Pre-departure telephone service was also available, as it had been since 1905. MUrray Hill 8000 would reach a passenger in Grand Central Terminal, WAbash 4200 at La Salle Street Station, and OXford 1029 in Boston.

The observation car had a "lounging room with moveable wicker chairs for ladies" (according to the brochure), along with a maid to "make all arrangements. These maids are also experienced manicurists." If the last car of the train catered especially to ladies, the first—the club car—was for the gentlemen. Stock quotations were posted there en route, as well as the "results of baseball games, American and National League, principal football games and other important sporting events." In 1928, obviously, gender roles were nothing if not clear.

The barber shop was in the club car, where men could get a shave for 30 cents, a haircut for 75, a shampoo for 50. Tonic was 25 cents extra, and the gentleman who wished his beard trimmed would pay 35 cents for that service. Actually, though the barber was located in the front-of-the-train male preserve, his services were unisex, offering to ladies—and this was unmistakably the age of the flapper—a straight bob for 75 cents or a shingle bob for $1. It was the barber who made arrangements for the shower bath at a charge of 50 cents. The valet service available in the club car also catered to both men and women: "Clothing sponged and pressed
continued on page 54

FACING PAGE, UPPER: **In this view from December 1931, the** *Advance 20th Century Limited* **is ready for departure, with patrons already settled in the lounge of the observation car. Hanging from the open platform, the tailsign glows blue with a glitter of marquee lights. This version of the famous carpet, buff with crimson borders, was introduced on the occasion of "The Cardinal's Train," a special section of the** *Century* **run in June 1926 to transport George Cardinal Mundelein to Chicago for an International Eucharistic Congress. NEW YORK CENTRAL**

FACING PAGE, LOWER: **It's April 24, 1932, the** *Century's* **timing is being dropped from 20 to 18 hours, and celebrities are on hand to witness the train's departure from Grand Central. New York City Mayor James K. Walker (who would never miss a party), Mr. and Mrs. William K. Vanderbilt, and New York Central president of a few months, Frederick E. Williamson, are among the notables. The press is there in force to record the occasion and celebrity attendance. NEW YORK CENTRAL**

RIGHT: This splendid 1938 photo of Grand Central Terminal with the elegant tower of the New York Central Building soaring behind shows the complex that stretched from 42nd to 46th streets as the planners intended it. To the left is the Biltmore Hotel; in the shadows to the right is the Commodore Hotel. Both were owned by NYC. Today the Biltmore is gone and the Commodore is but a skeleton inside the new Grand Hyatt. This northward view was destroyed when the PanAm Building was erected in 1963 between GCT and the New York Central Building. The undistinguished skyscraper was constructed on air rights sold by a New York Central sliding into bankruptcy. DAVID V. HYDE, NEW YORK CENTRAL

BELOW: Clearly posed, this picture speaks of the 1920s— fedoras for the men, a cloche hat for one stylish lady. These passengers are waiting for the first section of the *Century* at track 27. This was a usual *Century* gate in the halcyon days when the train almost always ran in multiple sections. NEW YORK CENTRAL

In this postcard view looking west toward the Vanderbilt Avenue entrance, Grand Central's concourse is bustling—but in a midday sort of way, without the surge of morning or afternoon commuters. Patrons buy their tickets at the windows to the left; the famous golden clock above the information kiosk remains prominent to this day. This view is not too far removed from 1947, Grand Central's busiest year, when it hosted 65 million travelers. WILLIAM F. HOWES JR. COLLECTION

TWENTIETH CENTURY LIMITED
GRAND CENTRAL TERMINAL

Beginning in February 1913, just a few years into the heavyweight era, the *20th Century Limited* had a launching pad in New York City in all ways worthy of that famous train's esteem — Grand Central Terminal, replacing on the same site the Grand Central Station that had been expanded and upgraded at the turn of the century. The new structure — through the years often called Grand Central Station, though "Terminal" was technically correct — was both a magnificent and monumental architectural statement and a brilliant piece of engineering, integrating rail, automobile, and pedestrian traffic in remarkably creative ways.

All the key pieces of the concept first came from the extraordinary mind of William J. Wilgus, who was New York Central & Hudson River's chief engineer at the time of GCT's planning. It was he who had overseen the upgrading of the railroad's physical plant just prior to the *Century's* inaugural. And it was he who planned the innovative Grand Central electrification, which was energized in 1906 and was the key to the GCT project. Along with eliminating the critical smoke problems that came with the steam locomotives that powered the 500 daily trains (not counting switching moves) that the old station hosted, electrification allowed the tracks to be placed underground — opening up for development the lucrative air rights above them, also Wilgus' vision.

Wilgus projected the two levels of tracks and platforms (the lower for suburban trains, the upper for long-distance), the loop tracks for turning, the ramps for fluid moving of pedestrians, the great concourse, the elevated roadway that straddles the building and links upper and lower Park Avenue, and the hotels — the Biltmore and the Commodore — that adjoined the station.

The architectural auspices of this extraordinary structure was complicated and cantankerous, but few have argued with the results. Reed & Stem of St. Paul, Minn., one of four firms initially submitting proposals, was hired, with Charles Reed (whose sister was married to Wilgus) instrumental in the terminal's overall design. Warren & Wetmore joined the team subsequently, with Whitney Warren (friend and cousin of William K. Vanderbilt, the Commodore's grandson and chairman of the board of the NYC&HR) largely responsible for the structure's monumental Beaux-Arts style.

Grand Central, which in the early years of the twenty-first century shines again in restored splendor, had and has many aspects that made it an uplifting and inspiring place to begin a journey. The vast main concourse is unforgettable, a towering and airy space flooded with light at certain times of day, with the sun streaming in through the five south-facing clerestory lunette windows. Here and in the also-imposing main waiting room, walls are of granite and limestone. In the center of the concourse is a round information booth capped by a four-faced golden clock — a favored meeting place for generations of New Yorkers.

On the lower level is the famous Oyster Bar, which through the years has offered all manner of seafood preparations, including its signature oyster pan roast. Ceilings in the main restaurant and counter areas are arched, finished in cream-colored terra-cotta tiles popularized by Spanish artisan Raphael Guastavino. Outside the Oyster Bar, also under a Guastavino arch, is the "whispering gallery," an acoustic curiosity that allows lovers — facing into the corners and many yards distant from each other — to speak perfectly audible sweet nothings to each other.

But no detail of GCT is more memorable than the concourse's vast cerulean blue ceiling, ornamented with 2,500 stars and the gilt outlines of constellations. Sixty of the stars are electric lights of variable intensity, reflecting the magnitude of the stars they represent. And for reasons still not entirely clear, the zodiac is depicted backwards — a mirror image of what we see if we look skyward.

All in all, Grand Central Terminal, where for decades the red carpet was rolled out for the *20th Century Limited*, was the perfect home for the perfect train with the perfect name.

over night: Suit (3-piece) $1.25 . . . skirt (plain) 75¢, (pleated) $1.25."

There was also a mailbox in the club car. "Letters stamped and deposited therein will be posted at the earliest opportunity to insure prompt delivery. Letters may also be handed to the stenographer for posting." The *Century*, of course, was a post office itself, and a "Via *20th Century*" designation for letters carried the urgency that "Via Air Mail" would a generation later. Many a Wall Street-area stationery store stocked red-and-blue Dennison labels for *20th Century* mail, and other letters arrived at the train marked with rubber stamps. A good deal of commercial paper—bank notes, stock certificates and such—traveled in the railway post office cars of Nos. 25 and 26 as well.

Ever since the railroads moved reluctantly into the dining-car business in the latter part of the nineteenth century, diners were the premier showcases of the best passenger trains. Railroads conceded that, though they would inevitably be money-losers, dining cars could also be great magnets for business, and they strove to offer fine, distinctive meals served in a style equal to that found in the best hotel dining rooms. The *Century* was by no means unique in laying its tables with fine linen, brightly polished hotel-grade silver, quality crystal, and vases of fresh flowers. But standards there were just a tad higher: no darned napery, no dented hollowware, no mediocre personnel.

Although most of the passenger-service crew aboard the *Century* were Pullman employees, the diner was staffed by NYC—and generously and expertly staffed at that. Working a 36-seat diner (with six each of tables for two and tables for four) were seven waiters under the direction of a steward, with a chef and three assistant cooks in the galley. Each member of this team would have his particular responsibilities: one to arrive early and start the coal fire in the range, another to polish the silver each night, another to see to beverages, and so forth.

New York Central dining-car service was headquartered in Buffalo, by the late 1920s in the impressive new Central Terminal, and the dining-car manager based there had a fleet of 156 dining cars under his care and direction. In this era the "Lines East" and "Lines West" demarcation—with Buffalo as the dividing point—was still strong, a holdover no doubt of the New York Central & Hudson River and Lake Shore & Michigan Southern duality. Lines East diners rarely ventured west, and vice-versa. Diners and their crews were still typically switched out en route—a practice then suspended only in the coldest months, since the cars often froze up waiting to be added to the trains in the wee hours, but soon to be abandoned entirely. Westbound, the diner from New York City left the *Century* consist at Syracuse and another joined it at Toledo, in time for early breakfasters. Eastbound the diner was switched out at Ashtabula, Ohio, and another switched in at Albany—at least two, actually, including one for the Boston section. Westbound, the Boston section's diner was switched out at Springfield, Mass.

The *20th Century's* departure from Grand Central during this period was at 2:45 P.M., while a regularly scheduled *Advance 20th Century Limited* left at 1:45 P.M., carded all the way to Chicago exactly

one hour ahead of the main train. Departures from La Salle Street were at 11:40 A.M. and 12:40 P.M. Since the dining car would open 15 minutes or more before departure, there was luncheon business in both directions, but far more eastbound.

Meals aboard the *Century* were always something special, though they changed through the years as culinary tastes evolved and expectations shifted. Early in the train's history the passenger would find an extensive á la carte listing. A sample dinner menu from 1912 had options arrayed under these headings: HORS D'OEUVRES; FROM THE GRILL; EGGS; OMELETTES; VEGETABLES; SALADS, COLD MEATS, ETC.: BREADS, ETC.; FRUIT AND DESSERTS; CHEESE; and TEA, COFFEE, ETC. The only slightly exotic offering on this menu was canapes with Russian caviar.

Midway through the heavyweight era, styles had changed, and the railroad featured a "blue plate service": an entree combined with appropriate potato and vegetable. These specials changed at least weekly and were different on Lines West and Lines East, eliminating duplication for round-trip passengers. The "Century Dinner" in 1927 cost $1.50 and offered such options as planked lake trout, broiled sweetbreads, and individual chicken pot pies. Those who preferred to dine in their own accommodations had that option too. "Passengers desiring meal service in their rooms or berths will confer a favor upon the management," read the informational brochure, "by notifying porter approximate time they would like their dinner served."

All this service, of course, came at a price. Throughout the 1920s, an extra fare of $9.60 was levied, with a potential refund of $1.20 per hour for late arrival, up to the total amount of the extra fare. Like the train's schedule, which bounced from 20 hours to as few as 15 hours and 45 minutes, changing some 20 times in the *Century's* 65-year career, extra-fare amounts and provisions went up and down. At the inauguration in 1902 the surcharge was $8, with a rebate of $1 an hour for lateness up to a total of $4. The extra fare was moved to $10 (the most it would ever be) in 1908, and again in 1932, when the refund provision was dropped for good. Tinkering continued, with the surcharge dropping to as low as $3 during World War II.

Since the *Century* was known for its proliferation of sections in the heavyweight era, the railroad felt compelled to publish this caveat in its informational brochure: "The *20th Century Limited* and other New York

Central passenger trains are frequently operated in two or more sections. It is therefore necessary that friends who plan to wire you en route or meet you at stations, should know the number of your Pullman car as well as the number or name of your train."

The burgeoning of sections peaked in 1927 when an extraordinary 2,261 were operated—an average of more than three per day in each direction. The following year the number dropped to 2,151, but for a reason that reflected strength, not weakness. In 1928, 95 percent of those myriad sections of the *Century* operated on time, and the train grossed more than $11 million—the most it ever had or ever would.

A simple motive-power fact lay behind all these numbers: the slight drop in sections operated, the remarkable on-time percentage and the record gross income. Nineteen twenty-eight was the first full year that the *Century* was pulled by the magnificent J-class Hudsons. These extraordinary locomotives, eventually 210 strong, were emblematic of the New York Central and of the *20th Century Limited* in many of its greatest years. Elegantly proportioned racehorses, these high-drivered 4-6-4s were named for the Central's great river. The "class engine" was J1a No. 5200, a prototype, experimental locomotive delivered in February 1927. It would be the sole member of the first of nine subclasses built over the next 11 years for New York Central and subsidiaries Michigan Central, Big

Behind J1d Hudson No. 5303, the *Century* stands ready to roll from La Salle Street Station in Chicago, with the Art Deco Board of Trade Building towering in the background. It's September 23, 1930, and the train is still on a 20-hour schedule, even though the more powerful Hudsons have replaced the K3 Pacifics. This schedule, in effect on-and-off since the train's inauguration in 1902, required an average speed of 48.3 miles per hour including stops, 52.2 miles per hour excluding them. OTTO C. PERRY, WESTERN HISTORY DEPARTMENT, DENVER PUBLIC LIBRARY

Four, and Boston & Albany. All would be constructed by Schenectady-based American Locomotive Company (Alco) except B&A's ten J2c's, which were products of Lima Locomotive Works of Lima, Ohio.

When he took over as Central's chief engineer of motive power and rolling stock on January 1, 1926, Paul W. Kiefer was presented with a problem. The Central's passenger business had outstripped the capabilities of the evolving fleet of 4-6-2s that had hauled the "Great Steel Fleet" for many years. Nine cars were the limit for a K3 Pacific, which meant running many trains in multiple sections. The challenge: Without exceeding existing clearances and weight restrictions, design a locomotive able to haul 12 to 14 heavyweight Pullmans. Kiefer and his staff were up to that challenge, and the glorious Hudsons were born. They were the first 4-6-4s ever built, and their four-wheel trailing trucks allowed bigger fireboxes and boilers and spread the increased weight over more axles. Not only were they efficient, they were beautiful. They were a splendid match for a dignified train.

In 1930 the Central published a slim volume by Edward Hungerford called *The Run of the Twentieth Century*. As a journalist and later an impresario, Hungerford made a career of glorifying trains—which he did very, very effectively. His first big splash came in 1927 when he produced, for the Baltimore & Ohio Railroad on the occasion of its centennial, the Fair of the Iron Horse, a parade of historical equipment that embraced live theater and music. He created a number of similar transportation pageants through the 1930s, including ones in Rochester, Syracuse, and Cleveland—all New York Central cities. The decade culminated in his grand "Railroads on Parade," with music by Kurt Weill, at the 1939–40 New York World's Fair. "Wheels a-Rolling" for the 1948–49 Chicago Railroad Fair was the last of his pageants.

All this came long after Hungerford had written *The Run of the Twentieth Century*, of course. Though there's no getting around the fact that the book is essentially company propaganda, it is engagingly written and rich with fascinating, first-hand details (many of which have found their way into this account and those of other chroniclers) about running an operation of the scope and complexity of the *Century*, where excellence is always the assumption. In his epic, the *20th Century Limited* ran freighted with expectations.

"An expression of our American life today," he called the *Century*, "of its virility, of its force, of its unending demand for speed, precision, comfort." Though this vision is perhaps overblown, Hungerford did make a good case for it. The dimension, consistency, and attention to detail in an enterprise that sent as many as seven *20th Century Limited*s a day (in a single direction) streaking across the landscape of the Northeast did indeed have a heroic aspect. And the beautifully proportioned Hudsons were just the right locomotives to fit his heroic vision.

If services and reputation changed little over the *Century*'s 28 years as a heavyweight train, the cars themselves were a fluid proposition, evolving as technology improved and tastes changed—in favor, for instance, of private rooms over open sections. Some of the most luxurious Pullmans ever built were the *Valley*-series observations, a dozen of which arrived in April 1929 for the *Century*. Carrying such names as

The *Valley*-series observations, a dozen of which were built in 1929 for the *20th Century Limited*, were truly elegant cars, among the finest to carry the flagship's markers in any era. The following July, four identical cars—*Genesee Valley*, *Schoharie Valley*, *Seneca Valley*, and *Tioga Valley*—were delivered by Pullman for the *Southwestern Limited*, a train that during that era was virtually the *Century*'s equal. These photos are of *Seneca Valley*. The elegance of the cars' interior finish is evidenced here, along with the brightness that stems from the extra-tall windows and light walls and ceiling. From roughly 1910 into the 1940s, John Peter Van Voorst was the Pullman Company photographer; you can see his initials inked on negatives of all Pullman builder's photos—a blended J. P. followed by V. V. BOTH PHOTOS, THE PULLMAN COMPANY, PETER V. TILP COLLECTION

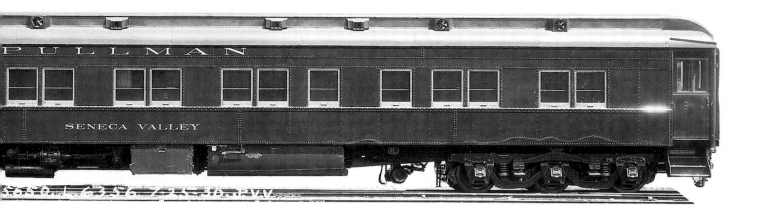

Hudson Valley, Oswego Valley, Sandusky Valley, Tonawanda Valley, and *Seneca Valley,* these cars featured just one drawing room and one single bedroom, which could be opened en suite to create a truly princely accommodation. In addition to a generous lounge in the forward section of the car, there was a fine-looking, clubby room at the other end, with tall windows for optimum viewing, extensive stenciling for elegance, and overstuffed chairs for comfort.

The *Valley* cars' immediate predecessors were fine vehicles, too: the 15 *Central*-series 3-compartment 2-drawing room observation-lounges from 1925. These cars carried such non-NYC-related names as *Central Avenue* and *Central City.* (That one was named *Central Park* probably had more to do with coincidence than with New York City.) Among the first heavyweight observations to run on Nos. 25 and 26 were a group of nine 8-compartment observation-lounges built in 1911. Their names—*Conneaut, Farnham, Fontanet, Geneva, Painesville, Waldameer, Watertown, Waynesport,* and *Westboro*—recognized generally obscure towns in New York Central territory, but predated the practice of naming cars in series form. (The next generation of yardmasters, passenger department planners, and other railroaders would know instantly the configuration of a car with which they were dealing when they saw, for example, the word "Valley" or "Central" in its name.)

The sleeping-car staple dating well back into the wooden-car era was the "twelve-and-one"—the car with 12 open sections (upper and lower berths partitioned from the aisle by heavy curtains) and one drawing room, the premier accommodation. On the *Century* in the later heavyweight years, the 12-1s were typified by the *East*-series cars of 1925: *East Buffalo, East Syracuse, East Toledo,* and so on. Other late entries were the 14-section *Star-* and *New*-series Pullmans—informally called "stag" cars, since they were patronized largely by men traveling alone, typically on business.

Through the 1920s, however, the popularity of open sections waned, and upper berths in particular became increasingly difficult to sell. This resulted in the typical *Century* consist's including cars with more private rooms, or even all-room cars. In this latter category were the 20 *Glen*-series

Private Bedrooms with Real Beds

The New York Central has in service on a number of the through trains of the Great Steel Fleet, private bedroom cars that provide room accommodations at a substantial saving in cost. It will pay you to make inquiry regarding this service the next time you are making a trip on any of the trains on which these cars are run.

These rooms are in reality private bedrooms in which you enjoy a real bed, longer than an ordinary lower berth, with soft mattress and deep box springs for your restful sleep on the Water Level Route.

Each room, arranged crosswise in the car, has a toilet, lavatory, electric fan, vacuum bottle, a folding shelf conveniently used as writing desk or a breakfast table, and an attractively designed reading lamp.

Bedroom cars on the "Advance 20th Century," the "20th Century" and "The Commodore Vanderbilt" between New York and Chicago, "The Detroiter" between New York and Detroit, and the "Toronto Limited" and "The Maple Leaf" between New York and Toronto, have convertible beds affording a comfortable sofa lounge for day travel. If two persons occupy the room an upper berth may be let down. Bedroom cars on other trains have stationary beds and no upper berths.

The charge for single occupancy is only one quarter more than the regular fare plus double the lower berth charge. The charge for double occupancy is two regular fares plus double the lower berth charge.

All the conveniences of a first class hotel

Convertible by day into a comfortable sofa lounge Double Bedroom Car

All ready to drop into for your night's sleep

Breakfast in comfort before leaving the train

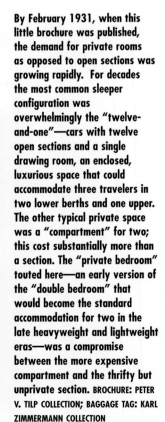

By February 1931, when this little brochure was published, the demand for private rooms as opposed to open sections was growing rapidly. For decades the most common sleeper configuration was overwhelmingly the "twelve-and-one"—cars with twelve open sections and a single drawing room, an enclosed, luxurious space that could accommodate three travelers in two lower berths and one upper. The other typical private space was a "compartment" for two; this cost substantially more than a section. The "private bedroom" touted here—an early version of the "double bedroom" that would become the standard accommodation for two in the late heavyweight and lightweight eras—was a compromise between the more expensive compartment and the thrifty but unprivate section. BROCHURE: PETER V. TILP COLLECTION; BAGGAGE TAG: KARL ZIMMERMANN COLLECTION

6-compartment 3-drawing room Pullmans, delivered in 1928 for *Century* service, with names like *Glen Adair* and *Glen Terrace*. In 1929 came six *Willow*-series 7-drawing room cars. (As a super-luxury train, the *20th Century* actually had all-room cars for most of the heavyweight era, including five 10-compartment cars dating from 1914: *Highland Falls*, *Niagara Falls*, *Port Clinton*, *River View*, and *Spuyten Duyvil*.) There were also 8-section 2-compartment 1-drawing room Pullmans.

From the always-evolving rich stew of heavyweight Pullmans came the assemblage of *20th Century Limited* consists throughout the teens and twenties—consists tailored on a daily basis to meet requests for space. As demand grew along with the train's fame, the *Century* proliferated into multiple sections for each departure.

One indication of the prominence of the Central's flagship in the American consciousness was the Broadway debut in 1932 of "Twentieth Century," an antic farce by Ben Hecht and Charlie MacArthur. (Just four years earlier they had opened "The Front Page," a hugely successful and often revived comedy-drama about the newspaper business.) "Twentieth Century" was indirectly a tribute to its namesake train, since the play's action was set at Chicago's La Salle Street Station, at the train gate in Grand Central Terminal's concourse, and aboard a heavyweight Pullman, with both sections and lounge depicted in extraordinary verisimilitude.

The madcap plot involved egomaniacal theater impresario Oscar Jaffe (Moffat Johnson) and a glamorous Russian stage star, his ex-mistress (Eugenie Leontovich). By chance, they meet aboard the *20th Century*—a train that in real life, of course, had become a great favorite of theater and movie people—and the fireworks begin. Hecht and MacArthur (husband of actress Helen Hayes) started with the premise that the *Century* was simply too stuffy in its moral tone and expectations in dress and decorum, which they thought could be a source of fun. This led Hecht to the idea of bringing aboard an actor who plays Christ in a touring

This picture of the eastbound *Century* at Elkhart, Ind., on September 9, 1928, does indeed show two sections of the train. But the section at the right, pulling out of the station, is actually the second. The one waiting to go, behind J1b Hudson 5228, built in 1927, is the third. The first section is already scorching the ballast en route to New York City. A. W. JOHNSON, PETER V. TILP COLLECTION

61

version of the Oberammergau Passion Play, along with theater types that were easily recognizable to Broadway insiders. (Jaffe, as railway author Lucius Beebe reported, was a synthesis of David Belasco and Morris Gest.)

If the characters were true-to-life, so were the sets. The Grand Central train gate (track 27, which the *Century* typically used in that era) was a dead ringer for the original. The Pullman was no less perfect, with the compartment's convertible seats, the light fixtures, the moldings, the window arrangement, the stenciling, the upholstery all just right. Redcaps, porters, and conductor all were accurately costumed. When a blanket was a prop, it was recognizably a Pullman blanket. "Railroad buffs and spies from the New York Central could detect no flaws behind the footlights," according to Beebe.

In 1934 the play was made into a movie starring John Barrymore as Jaffe and Carole Lombard as Lily Garland, a chorine that he transforms into a leading lady and then alienates. The movie naturally reached a wider audience. Though the screenplay was also written by Hecht and MacArthur, it took some liberties with the original.

By the mid 1930s, though, change was at hand for the *20th Century Limited*. Streamlining was in the wind, and the Central was looking to reequip its flagship in this mode. Planning to this end was intensive and ongoing. A harbinger of what was to come was the *Commodore Vanderbilt*, a Hudson given streamlined shrouding in 1934 that routinely appeared on the *Century* (and even more frequently in publicity for it) in the train's late heavyweight years.

This posed picture of J1c Hudson No. 5271 with the *20th Century Limited* in tow along the Hudson River at Breakneck, N.Y., is classic and commanding. The elegant simplicity of the smokebox, the drop coupler in the pilot, the flags waving in a breeze not motion-generated, the wisp of steam from the cylinder cocks—everything is stately and heroic. This is clearly a train in which you could believe. NEW YORK CENTRAL, PETER V. TILP COLLECTION

FACING PAGE (BROCHURE COVER): The reduction in the *Century*'s timing to 16½ hours is a harbinger of the all-streamlined train that is less than three years away, and so is the streamlined Hudson named *Commodore Vanderbilt* featured on the cover of the announcement of that schedule tightening. Other trains—the *Commodore Vanderbilt*, *Wolverine*, *North Shore Limited*, *Niagara*, and *Southwestern Limited*—also had their schedules trimmed at this time. MIKE SCHAFER COLLECTION

TWENTIETH CENTURY LIMITED

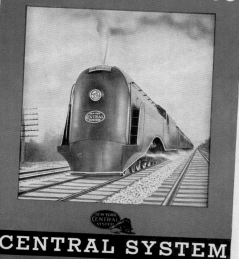

IMPORTANT
TRAVEL
NEWS

EFFECTIVE SUNDAY
September 29, 1935

. . . . . . The Century, for 33 years the leading passenger train between New York and Chicago and the best known train in the world, again makes railroad history by cutting another half hour from its schedule, making the running time in both directions 16½ hours.

The business man closes his desk on the day's work before departure and arrives in either city when the business day begins.

The Century represents the best in rail transportation. It is completely Air-Conditioned and embodies every provision for comfort and safety.

WESTBOUND
Lv. New York . . . 5:30 P.M.
Lv. Boston . . . . 3:00 P.M.
Ar. Chicago . . . 9:00 A.M.

EASTBOUND
Lv. Chicago . . . 3:30 P.M.
Ar. New York . . 9:00 A.M.
Ar. Boston . . . . 11:30 A.M.

NEW YORK CENTRAL SYSTEM

20TH
Century Limited
16½ HOURS
Between
NEW YORK ● CHICAGO

THE WATER LEVEL ROUTE ● YOU CAN SLEEP

STREAMLINED PIONEER

Railroad streamlining is generally considered to date from early 1934, when Chicago, Burlington & Quincy and Union Pacific launched their and M-10000 pocket streamliners powered by internal combustion. But it was New York Central that claimed primacy in streamlining a steam locomotive.

"World's first streamlined high-powered steam locomotive" was the railroad's no doubt accurate claim for its *Commodore Vanderbilt*, a sheet-metal streamlining of Hudson No. 5344 at the railroad's West Albany shops. (Though 5344 was the last of the J1e-class Hudsons, its selection for this honor was apparently random; it just happened to be in the shops in the fall of 1934.)

The *Commodore Vanderbilt*'s handsome shrouding, created by Carl Kantola, was meant to have aerodynamic benefits, and the shape had undergone wind-tunnel testing at Case Institute in Cleveland. But publicity quite certainly had been the real motivation behind its creation, and not long after its December 1934 roll-out it was towed to Grand Central Terminal for display. According to historian Peter Tilp, the locomotive was discovered to be slightly too tall to fit through the Park Avenue tunnel into the station. Kantola suggested filling the boiler completely with water—which worked. The extra weight compressed the springs just enough to let the locomotive slip in.

Painted in gun-metal-gray lacquer, with running boards and the curve of the skirting outlined in silver, the *Commodore Vanderbilt* was understated and elegant. In fact, in hues and style, it set a direction and aesthetic that Henry Dreyfuss would take to its quintessence in his *20th Century Limited* of 1938. The locomotive's first revenue assignment, beginning in February 1935, was to haul the *Century* between Chicago and Toledo—a stint which lasted eight months.

In mid-1939 No. 5344 was re-streamlined in the style Dreyfuss had by then created for the *Century* and went into service between Chicago and Detroit on the *Mercury*.

Though the *20th Century Limited* featured in this brochure depicts a heavyweight train, the publication's style says "streamlining"—not just in the inclusion of the shrouded *Commodore Vanderbilt* Hudson on the cover, but in the lettering and graphics as well. Inside, there's a long testimonial from Lady Mabel Dunn, "well-known English music critic," who had ridden the *Century*: "Writing as a traveler in many lands, this to my mind embodies perfection— for all that the average traveler can ask, or really cares about, is safe, fast, luxurious and effortless transportation."
PETER V. TILP COLLECTION

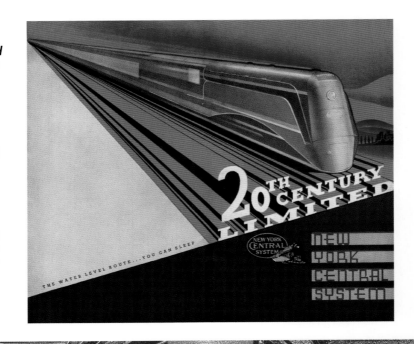

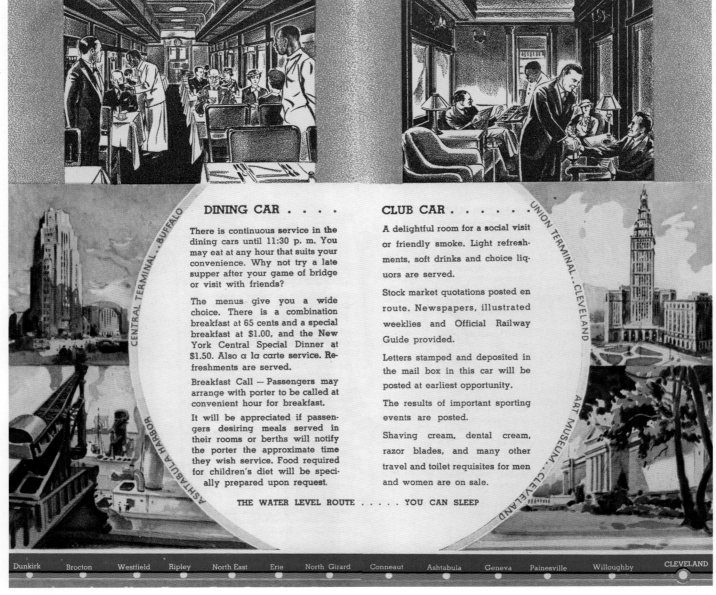

DINING CAR . . . .

There is continuous service in the dining cars until 11:30 p. m. You may eat at any hour that suits your convenience. Why not try a late supper after your game of bridge or visit with friends?

The menus give you a wide choice. There is a combination breakfast at 65 cents and a special breakfast at $1.00, and the New York Central Special Dinner at $1.50. Also a la carte service. Refreshments are served.

Breakfast Call — Passengers may arrange with porter to be called at convenient hour for breakfast.

It will be appreciated if passengers desiring meals served in their rooms or berths will notify the porter the approximate time they wish service. Food required for children's diet will be specially prepared upon request.

CLUB CAR . . . . . .

A delightful room for a social visit or friendly smoke. Light refreshments, soft drinks and choice liquors are served.

Stock market quotations posted en route. Newspapers, illustrated weeklies and Official Railway Guide provided.

Letters stamped and deposited in the mail box in this car will be posted at earliest opportunity.

The results of important sporting events are posted.

Shaving cream, dental cream, razor blades, and many other travel and toilet requisites for men and women are on sale.

THE WATER LEVEL ROUTE . . . . . YOU CAN SLEEP

Dunkirk · Brocton · Westfield · Ripley · North East · Erie · North Girard · Conneaut · Ashtabula · Geneva · Painesville · Willoughby · CLEVELAND

Though two more glorious chapters remained in the *20th Century Limited* story, hindsight suggests that not even the splendid streamliners to come would ever quite equal the abundance and unquestioned ascendancy of the train in the heavyweight era. In the glory years of the heavyweight *Century*, when multiple sections were the rule, the greatest single day had come on January 7, 1929, when seven eastbound sections carried 822 revenue passengers. The occasion for this peak in business was the National Automobile Show, held in New York City. The handwriting was on the wall, for those who could read it.

4

HENRY DREYFUSS' ELEGANT STREAMLINER

n June 15, 1938, New York Central's latest version of its *20th Century Limited* stood poised to open another chapter in a story then exactly 36 years old (June 15 was again the date of choice for an inaugural of the *Century*). This new chapter was streamlining *à la* Henry Dreyfuss; the story was one of already established preeminence.

The consists waiting on that afternoon would do nothing to dim this luster. At Grand Central Terminal in New York and at Chicago's La Salle Street Station, the streamlined *20th Century Limited*—trains

In a rare color view captured on July 2, 1940, the westbound *Century* has just passed Peekskill and is headed into the Highlands of the Hudson. The lush green of Bear Mountain is just a few miles away, and the gray stone of Storm King Mountain not too many more. It's a beautiful early summer evening, perfect for enjoying these fine sights. Less than two years old, the train still has an aura of newness. HERBERT H. HARWOOD SR., HERBERT H. HARWOOD JR. COLLECTION

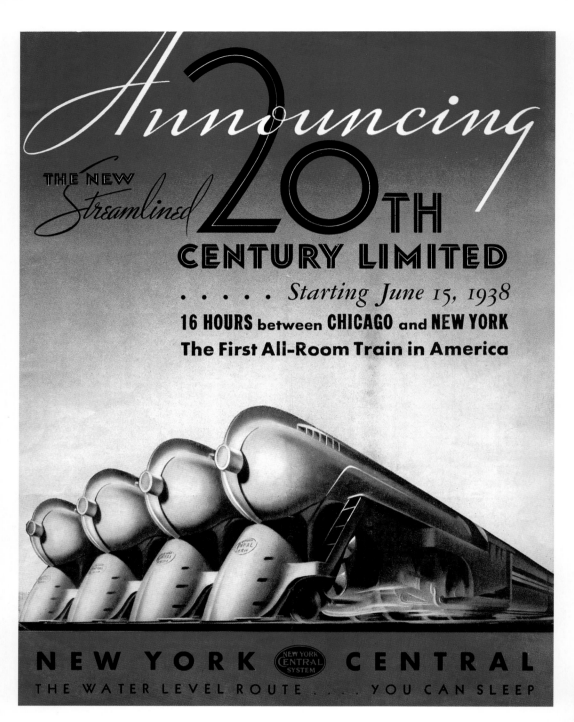

Announcing

THE NEW *Streamlined* 20TH CENTURY LIMITED

. . . . . Starting June 15, 1938

16 HOURS between CHICAGO and NEW YORK

The First All-Room Train in America

NEW YORK *NEW YORK CENTRAL SYSTEM* **CENTRAL**

THE WATER LEVEL ROUTE . . . . . YOU CAN SLEEP

25 and 26—shone in exquisite, understated elegance. The Dreyfuss color scheme was cool and clean: a blue-edged dark gray band on a background of lighter gray, with twin silver stripes at window level.

Just blocks away in both cities—at New York's Pennsylvania Station and Chicago's Union—the competition lurked: Pennsylvania Railroad's new, streamlined *Broadway Limited*, styled by Raymond Loewy and ready to be inaugurated simultaneously to the minute with the *Century*. Pennsy and Central were, of course, the fiercest of competitors, so once again a significant change in their passenger services ran exactly parallel. Neither railroad was willing to concede an edge.

This lent an air of collaboration to the *Broadway/20th Century* venture. Perhaps because Pullman would build and own most of the cars involved in the 1938 streamliners—which for Pennsy included an entire "Fleet of Modernism," not only the *Broadway Limited* but also

68

the *Liberty Limited*, "*Spirit of St. Louis*," and *The General*—they were often spoken of together.

The first official word of the project, for instance, was a joint statement by the two railroads on March 9, 1937, that staff engineers and industrial designers were working on new equipment that "will mark a distinct departure from that now in service. While it will preserve the advantage of spaciousness afforded by standard-size Pullman cars, it will embody many novel features of interior design, decoration, and arrangement." The announcement also predicted the reduction of running time for the *Broadway* and *Century* from the existing 16½ hours to 16 even, which would require an average speed of nearly 60 miles per hour including intermediate stops.

Pullman Inc., formed in 1927, remained an important force in the evolution of the NYC and PRR 1938 streamliners. Pullman-Standard—the company's construction arm—would build all 104 all-room sleeping and lounge cars, 52 for each railroad. The Pullman Company, yet another branch of Pullman Inc., owned and staffed those cars. P-S also supplied six diners and four mail-baggage cars for the *Century*. Thus these trains—the *Century* and PRR's Fleet of Modernism—are a remarkable invitation to

Here, a Hudson treads where it may never have before and probably never would again— the electrified Terminal Division into Grand Central. The occasion was the train's display there just prior to its June 15, 1938, inaugural. Of the ten streamlined Hudsons, half were equipped with Scullin disc drivers and half with Boxpok. Number 5455, seen here, has disc drivers.
ED NOWAK, NEW YORK CENTRAL,
PETER V. TILP COLLECTION

compare and contrast the styles and aesthetics of the two roads. Since the cars were manufactured simultaneously by the same builder, they shared most technical and mechanical innovations. And, the trains would offer basically similar accommodations and services.

If one train had a barbershop (it did), then the other certainly had better have one. The same went for radios in the lounges and on-board secretarial services. And while the trade press generally lumped the projects together and reported them as one entity, the reader of one railroad's brochures and publicity would have no idea that a competitor even existed. "First all-room train in America" trumpeted the Central of its *20th Century Limited*. "The *Broadway Limited* now departs as a magnificent all-room train, the first in history," ballyhooed Pennsy. Technically, because of the trains' absolutely simultaneous births, both claims were true.

Yet another example of the joint aegis of the streamliner project was the presentation made on June 13, two days before the trains' inaugurations,

The *20th Century Limited* on pre-inaugural display at La Salle Street Station in Chicago in June 1938 presents a remarkable portrait of streamlining by Henry Dreyfuss—a study in grays, with subtle accents of aluminum and blue. Some 40,000 visitors inspected the train. There was no red carpet rollout, a tradition that had long been established at the New York end of the run but which did not appear at La Salle Street until after World War II, and relatively briefly. Partly visible through the observation-car windows is the display case featuring a model of the Dreyfuss-style Hudson and a speedometer. PHIL AND BEV BIRK COLLECTION

by Chicago's Mayor Kelley. In a single ceremony, four honorary plaques were awarded. One recipient was Chicago-based carbuilder Pullman-Standard (although the Budd Company built two diners for PRR, which also rebuilt some heavyweight equipment in its own shops for use on the Fleet of Modernism). The Pullman Company, which would operate the cars, was also honored, as were the two railroads. The presentation was part of pre-inaugural festivities, which included equipment exhibits on both June 13 and 14.

In New York, an estimated 65,000 visitors inspected the twin 13-car consists of the *20th Century*, which stood on tracks 36 and 37 of Grand Central's upper level. (Since locomotives under steam were not allowed into the electrified Park Avenue Tunnel and Grand Central Terminal, the J3s' fires were banked and the trains pulled in and out by decidedly unstreamlined T2a electric "motors"—quite a contrast to the sleek Hudsons.) The 12-piece Grand Central Terminal Redcap Orchestra played

popular tunes. Stamp collectors could buy special envelopes with inaugural seals, to be carried and postmarked aboard the initial run, and postcards were available as well. At Chicago's La Salle Street Station, an impressive 40,000 or so visitors came to look—quite a number, considering that streamliners, although a novelty for New Yorkers, were becoming almost old hat for Chicagoans.

It was in Chicago, back in February 1934, that the first streamliner—Union Pacific's M-10000—had begun its exhibition tour. Then, in May, Burlington's *Zephyr* 9900 had ended its dramatic nonstop demonstration run from Denver on the stage of the Century of Progress Exposition in Chicago. After that, *Zephyr*s from Chicago had proliferated: the *Twin Zephyr*s to Minneapolis-St. Paul in 1935 and the *Denver Zephyr* in 1936. So had *City* streamliners, which at the time left town on the Chicago & North

Western, bound for the Union Pacific at Omaha: the *City of Portland* in 1935 and the *City of Los Angeles, City of San Francisco,* and *City of Denver* in 1936.

Also in 1935, the Milwaukee Road's Otto Kuhler-style streamlined *Hiawatha*s began speeding between Chicago and the Twin Cities. Baltimore & Ohio-controlled Alton Railroad's *Abraham Lincoln* had that year brought streamlining to the Chicago–St. Louis route. The following year these endpoints gained a competitor streamliner: Illinois Central's *Green Diamond.* In 1937, Alton added the *Ann Rutledge,* formerly B&O's original streamlined *Royal Blue.*

Rock Island's streamliners hit the rails in 1937, offering two services from Chicago: the *Peoria Rocket* and the *Des Moines Rocket.* Also that year, Santa Fe inaugurated the streamlined *Super Chief,* and finally, in the early months of 1938—just ahead of Pennsy and New York Central—added more glitter to Chicago's Dearborn Station with additional streamliners: *El Capitan,* the *Chief,* the *Chicagoan/Kansas Cityan.*

In streamliners at least, Chicago was by no means the "second city" but rather enjoyed a clear preeminence. In comparison, the New York City area could only claim Baltimore & Ohio's Washington–Jersey City *Royal Blue* (1935) and Reading's Philadelphia–Jersey City *Crusader* (1937). Generally speaking, the Northeast was not notably streamliner country in the early years, although two were inaugurated in 1935. Boston & Maine had the *Zephyr* 9900-clone *Flying Yankee* connecting Bangor, Maine, and Boston, while the New Haven's *Comet* flew between Boston and Providence, R.I.

Of special note to our story of the 1938 streamlined *20th Century Limited* was the *Mercury,* New York Central's home-built streamliner, which initially ran between Cleveland and Detroit, beginning on July 15, 1936. This distinctive nine-car train was created at the railroad's Beech Grove Shops in Indiana from suburban coaches that had been built by Osgood Bradley in 1927. Everything, including the train's "bathtub"-shrouded Pacific-type steam locomotive (not entirely successful aesthetically) and the distinctive round-end observation car that author Lucius Beebe said looked like "the gunner's blister on a bombing plane," was designed by Henry Dreyfuss—his first project for the Central and, in fact, his first in railroading.

"Cleanlining" was the term Dreyfuss gave to his design concept and objective in general, whatever the application. His career in industrial design had

LEFT: Henry Dreyfuss, seen here working at his drafting board circa 1970, was among the most noted practitioners in the new field of industrial design. He styled tractors, appliances, clocks, telephones, ocean-liner interiors, and much more. His railroad commissions were few, but in his *20th Century Limited* Dreyfuss created one of the transportation industry's greatest icons. COURTESY OF STUART LEUTHNER

≡THE≡STREAMLINED
20TH CENTURY LIMITED
of the
NEW YORK CENTRAL SYSTEM

A picture of perfection is this publicity view of the *20th Century* rolling westbound with just a smudge of coal smoke hanging above the locomotive's boiler-top cowling. The sky is filled with fair-weather clouds, and the late-afternoon sun shines brightly and auspiciously for the New York Central's beautiful new streamliner. The future proved to be darker than this vision would suggest, however. World War II was just a few short years away, and the peaks in passenger-miles the *Century* reached in the late 1920s would not be equaled in the streamline era. NEW YORK CENTRAL, PHIL AND BEV BIRK COLLECTION

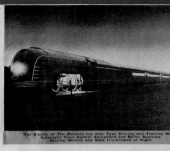
begun in 1929 when he was 25; before it ended with his death in 1972 (a joint suicide with his wife, who had been diagnosed with inoperable cancer of the liver), he would put his distinctive touch on many now-familiar objects. Though he eventually opened a California office and did much of his work there, Dreyfuss was a New Yorker through and through, so his work for the NYC was highly appropriate.

LEFT: The *Mercury*, named for the fleet-footed messenger god, was both New York Central's and Henry Dreyfuss' first streamliner. Initially a Cleveland–Detroit train (it was later extended west to Chicago), the *Mercury* was a silk purse created from a sow's ear. With Dreyfuss establishing the aesthetics, this train was created in the Central's shops from plain-vanilla suburban coaches nearly a decade old. The figure of Mercury is somewhat reminiscent of the more-famous image of Zephyrus, the god of the west wind, used by the Chicago, Burlington & Quincy.
KARL ZIMMERMANN COLLECTION

Manhattan-born, on March 2, 1904, and Brooklyn-raised, Dreyfuss won a two-year scholarship to Manhattan's Ethical Culture School, a well-deserved stroke of good fortune that set him on the career path he would so illustriously follow. For one thing, he took a course there in theatrical design from Norman Bel Geddes, who impressed him enormously—so much so that, after graduation, he went to work in Bel Geddes' office before setting up his own, on West 48th Street. Again following Bel Geddes' lead, he began to concentrate more and more on the emerging field of industrial design. He was encouraged in this shift by Doris Marks, an assistant in his office who in 1930 became his wife. For the next 42 years she would manage the business end of Dreyfuss' affairs—finances, contracts, and the like.

The "Big Ben" alarm clock for Westclox Company was among the most widely known Dreyfuss designs. In 1933 he moved the motor unit of the GE refrigerator from top to bottom; no more stooping to reach into the shelves. He worked on Hoover vacuum cleaners, John Deere & Company tractors, washing machines for Sears, Roebuck, and Royal typewriters. For seven years he designed covers and layouts for *McCalls* magazine.

...ervation Car of The Mercury

The parlor observation ...of The Mercury is an "Observation" car in ...ery sense of the word. The passengers' seats ...y be turned outward toward the broad win- ...ws while in the rounded observation end are ...o richly upholstered longitudinal settees and ...similar lounge facing the rear of the train. ...ssengers may obtain a full view of the passing ...nery. There is a special compartment for ...cking hand baggage, coats and parcels.

Special Whistle of Musical Tone Distinguishes The Mercury from Other Trains.

Coaches of The Mercury

The streamlined coaches of The Mercury are comfortable and reflect in every way the scheme of the entire train.

The seats are of the double rotating type with movable head rest covers. In the center are four built-in chairs facing each other with table and reading lamps between. The general illumination is indirect.

There is a smoking lounge for men and women equipped with semi-circular settees, loose chairs and tables.

Special attention has been given to the women's dressing room which is extra large, has separate toilet compartment and is fitted with dressing table, illuminated mirror, movable bench and other conveniences contributing to the comfort of women passengers.

The Floor Plan of Every Car of The Mercury is Individual, Giving the Appearance of a Succession of Rooms.

Parlor Car of The Mercury

In The Mercury parlor cars are large movable chairs, tables and reading lamps.

The warm colorings of tans, brown, rust and gold provide a restful background.

There is a distinctive and inviting drawing room, accommodating six persons, located mid- way of the car. There are built-in circular couches, tables, end lamps, coarse weave cur- tains, folding bridge tables and chairs, all con- tributing to the unique and pleasant settings.

Hand baggage and coats are cared for in a compartment provided specially for that purpose.

The Mercury Stops and Starts as a Unit. There is no Slack Between Cars. Wall Spaces Between Cars are Closed by New Diaphragm Closure.

ABOVE: The interior of the *Mercury*'s inaugural booklet shows off the stylishness of Dreyfuss' transformation of the Osgood Bradley commuter cars. Where only straight-back coach seats stood, there now were, for an additional fare, the comforts of a parlor car and a round-end parlor observation car with lots of glass. For those familiar with the color palette of Dreyfuss' later *20th Century Limited*, the hues of the Mercury may be surprising: "warm colorings of tans, brown, rust, and gold," according to the brochure. The dining car was full length, with the kitchen in the adjacent car. The diner was divided into three sections by edge-lighted etched-glass partitions; the center section had inward-facing banquettes, a novelty in dining-car seating that Dreyfuss would also use aboard the *Century*. KARL ZIMMERMANN COLLECTION

He styled the interiors of a pair of ocean liners launched in 1951: American Export's sisters, the *S. S. Constitution* and the *S. S. Independence*. At the 1939 World's Fair, he was responsible for the AT&T Company building and exhibits, as well as "Democracity," a presentation inside the Perisphere. And his streamlined J3a Hudson—No. 5453—was also on display. (His mentor, Bel Geddes, was prominently represented at the fair as well, with "Futurama," another miniature city, as was rival Raymond Loewy). The extent of his professional achievement became common knowledge when Dreyfuss appeared on the cover of the May 1, 1951, issue of *Forbes* magazine.

On the walls of both his New York City and Pasadena, Calif., offices hung this creed: "We bear in mind that the object we are working on is going to be ridden in, sat upon, looked at, talked into, activated, operated or in some way used by people. If the point of contact between the product and the people becomes a point of friction, then the industrial designer has failed. On the other hand, if people are made safe, more efficient, more comfortable—or just plain happier—by contact with the product, then the designer has succeeded."

Dreyfuss' responsibility for the *Mercury* had extended to all aspects of its design; in 1936 he was commissioned to work on the *20th Century* with the same all-embracing mandate. And this time he had more luck with the locomotive: ten J3a Hudsons that by general acclamation were judged the most aesthetically successful streamlined steam locomotives of all time. The train's exterior color scheme was his, as were the details of the interior design.

Then he worked on menus, crockery, glassware, finger-bowl liners, flatware, magazine covers, matchbooks, ashtrays, napkins, tickets, stationery—even the protective paper surrounding the lumps of sugar. Many of the objects bore the distinctive *20th Century Limited* logo:

continued on page 78

BELOW: This brochure dates from after the *Mercury*'s extension to Chicago in 1939. It features a different locomotive on the cover. In place of the train's original "bathtub" Pacific was a streamlined Hudson of the style done by Dreyfuss for the *Century*. Dreyfuss-designed Hudsons did see service on trains other than the *20th Century Limited*. KARL ZIMMERMANN COLLECTION

The **MERCURY**

CHICAGO · DETROIT
TOLEDO · CLEVELAND

NEW YORK CENTRAL SYSTEM

A ten-car *20th Century Limited*—somewhat shorter than the train's typical consist—glides south along the Hudson River during an
Albany–to–Harmon preview-trial run. E. L. DE GOLYER JR. PHOTOGRAPH COLLECTION, SOUTHERN METHODIST UNIVERSITY, DALLAS, TEXAS; COLLECTION ITEM NO. AG1982.232

continued from page 75

repeated horizontal bars underneath the train name, rendered in very clean, sans-serif lettering. One of the most arresting, elegant symbols ever associated with passenger railroading, this strikingly modern design was perhaps best known for its appearance on the observation car's tailsign, but it also turned up on the train's crockery and virtually all paper goods: menus, stationery, brochures, matchbooks, and the like. It was even woven into the famous red carpet that was rolled out on the platform for the *Century*'s departure from Grand Central right up until the end of the train's career.

"We wanted to give both comfort and speed without either being obvious," Dreyfuss said, "and I think we have achieved both."

To the extent that Dreyfuss and his *20th Century Limited* were ever criticized, it was for being too spare, cold, somewhat bloodless. Dreyfuss' competitor Raymond Loewy said that he suspected Dreyfuss was color-blind, a statement probably more catty than cogent. Still, gray is

The promotional brochure for the 1938 *Century* provided schedules for both the west- and eastbound trips as well as renderings that depicted the interiors of sleepers and feature cars, such as the club-lounge. The floor plans showed the variety of space—both sleeping accommodations and lounge and dining areas—incorporated by the 1938 *Century*. The traveler could book, from smallest to grandest, a roomette (for one),

WESTBOUND
SCHEDULE

	Daylight Saving Time	Standard Time
Lv. New York (Grand Central Terminal)	6:00 PM	5:00 PM
Lv. Harmon	h6:46 PM	h5:46 PM
Lv. Albany	h8:36 PM	h7:36 PM
Lv. Syracuse	h11:02 PM	h10:02 PM
Lv. Buffalo	h1:22 AM	h12:22 AM
Ar. Englewood	i8:46 AM	i7:46 AM
Ar. Chicago (La Salle St. Station)	9:00 AM	8:00 AM

h—Stops only to receive passengers.
i—Stops only to discharge passengers

ROOMETTE by Night
When you are ready to retire you merely lower the bed from the wall. Adjust the temperature and ventilation as you desire. You can sleep!

Copper metallic trim, brown cork v ture contribute to the rich harmony

MORE THAN EVER ••• IT PAYS

FLOOR PLAN OF THE VARIOUS TYPE

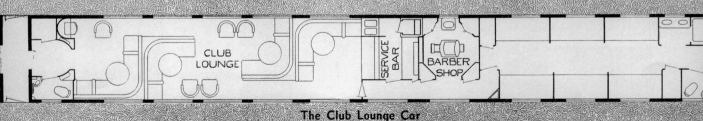

The Club Lounge Car

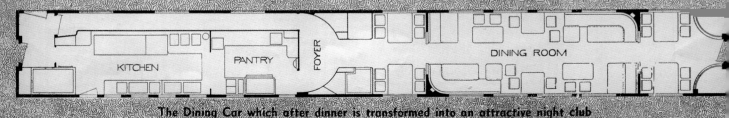

The Dining Car which after dinner is transformed into an attractive night club

78

surely the characteristic hue of Henry Dreyfuss' masterpiece for the New York Central.

The typical consist for the first section of the new, streamlined *20th Century* numbered 13 cars: a mail-baggage car, dormitory-buffet-lounge, two *City*-series 17-roomette sleepers, three *Imperial*-series 4-compartment 4-double-bedroom 2-drawing-room sleepers, two dining cars, two *Cascade*-series 10-roomette 5-double-bedroom sleepers, and an observation-lounge with a double bedroom and a master room. A total of 62 new cars were delivered for the *Century*, allowing for the operation of two sections in each direction at times of peak travel, with a dozen sleepers left over to run on the *Commodore Vanderbilt*, the *Detroiter*, the *Water Level Limited*, and the *Southwestern Limited*. A single section might swell to 16 or 17 cars with the addition of sleepers. The Central's total investment for this equipment—including the ten J3a's at $125,000 apiece—was nearly $6.2 million.

a double bedroom, a compartment, a drawing room (for three), or the single master room in the *Island*-series observation car. Passengers could socialize in the buffet-lounge at the head of the train, the observation car at the rear, or the dining car or cars in the middle. The portion of the two-color brochure shown on these two pages is reproduced at near actual size. ROBERT P. SCHMIDT COLLECTION

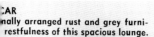

...ally arranged rust and grey furni-...restfulness of this spacious lounge.

THE CONVENIENT ROOMETTE
The roomette affords privacy and plenty of room in which to move around before retiring for the night and includes besides in-a-wall-bed, a clothes locker, lavatory and toilet.

EASTBOUND
SCHEDULE

	Daylight Saving Time	Standard Time
Lv. Chicago (La Salle St. Station)	4:00 PM	3:00 PM
Lv. Englewood	h4:10 PM	h3:10 PM
Lv. Toledo	h8:33 PM	h7:33 PM
Ar. Albany	i6:04 AM	i5:04 AM
Ar. Harmon	i8:00 AM	i7:00 AM
Ar. New York (Grand Central Terminal)	9:00 AM	8:00 AM

h—Stops only to receive passengers.
i—Stops only to discharge passengers.

TO RIDE THE CENTURY

...ARS THAT MAKE UP THE CENTURY

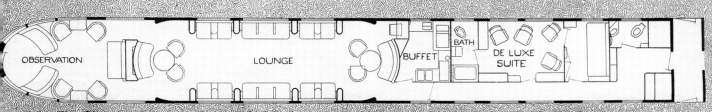

OBSERVATION — LOUNGE — BUFFET — BATH — DE LUXE SUITE

The Observation Lounge Car in which is located the de luxe suite consisting of bedroom and drawing room

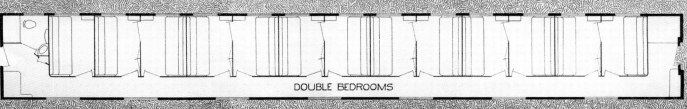

DOUBLE BEDROOMS

Sleeping Car with 13 double bedrooms

79

At the head of the train, right behind the mail-baggage, was the buffet-lounge, which also contained a barbershop and a crew dormitory sleeping 18. The lounge area of these cars—*Century Club*, *Century Inn*, *Century Lounge*, and *Century Tavern*—was described this way in a stunningly illustrated and designed booklet (most likely Henry Dreyfuss' work) prepared by and for the railroad to introduce its *20th Century*: "Copper metal trim, brown cork walls, and comfortable, informally arranged rust and gray furniture contribute to the rich harmony and satisfying restfulness of this smart, spacious room." The curved settees were arranged in a sort of maze pattern, breaking the corridor feel that is the *bête noir* of railroad-car interior design.

Even more handsome—and more unusual—were the six diners, Nos. 680–685, which rode on six-wheel trucks and cost about $92,000 each compared to an average of $78,000 for the various sleepers. They and the four baggage-RPOs were the only railroad-owned cars in the consist, all others belonging to The Pullman Company. Normal procedure was to run two diners, marshalled with dining areas adjacent. Windows in the dining-room car ends allowed passengers to look from one dining car into the other, thus creating the illusion of one long, continuous dining space. When the diners were run singly, drop mirrors covered the end windows.

Another novel feature of the diners was their use at night, after the dinner hour, as a nightclub. Bright lights were doused and an auxiliary system turned on, bathing the room in a soft, rosy glow. Rust-colored

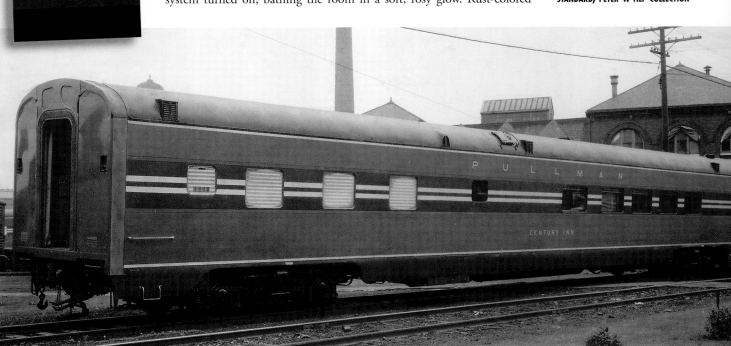

linen replaced white on the tables, and a radio or phonograph played swing-era music. But the dining car's main purpose, of course, was as Café Century, a rolling restaurant serving the breakfasts and dinners for which the train was so justly famous. (Notable entrees included Planked Spring Lamb Steak *20th Century*, Lobster Newburg, and Roast Shrewsbury Squab with guava jelly and a timbale of wild rice.) In those cars Dreyfuss indeed sought and achieved the feeling of a stylish restaurant. Again he eschewed the tunnel look of tradi-

BELOW: The rendering of the *Inn*-series cars that ran at the head of the train shows the "cleanlining" to which Henry Dreyfuss aspired in his designs.
JOE WELSH COLLECTION

Club Lounge . . . . .

THE PULLMAN COMPANY

LOUNGE CAR SERVICE

20TH CENTURY LIMITED

NEW YORK CENTRAL SYSTEM

Clean and simple, *Century* dining-car crockery repeated the stacked-bar design element. This cup and saucer is just one of several *Century* china items reproduced by Private Car Limited. **MIKE SCHAFER COLLECTION**

tional train interiors. At both ends of the room were "dinettes," each seating eight at two tables for four. In the main section, the facing corners had two banquettes. A smaller table adjoined each larger corner table; when placed together, they allowed five passengers to sit together, a real novelty aboard a dining car. There were additional tables for two, some with side-by-side seating, some with facing. The lock-step look of the traditional diner was successfully banished, yet the car could seat 38, a perfectly respectable number. (Diners typically seated either 36 or 48.)

The walls of the diner's main section were covered in gray leather, with mirrors in the panels between windows. The banquettes were likewise gray leather, but of a different texture, and the chairs rust-colored leather. In contrast, the dinette sections at the ends—separated from the main section by clear plastic partitions—had walls of walnut, ceilings of rust, and chairs upholstered in gray leather. At the end of the car, plants sat on quarter-circular walnut-veneered cabinets that held a linen locker, radio, and phonograph.

The eight Pullmans ahead of the observation car in the typical consist contained a mixture of drawing rooms, compartments, double bedrooms, and roomettes. These roomettes were the real novelty at the time, since they replaced open sections—the traditional curtain-draped upper and lower berths—making the *Century* (and the *Broadway*) the first all-room trains. Actually, to be misleadingly technical, the *Century* did carry

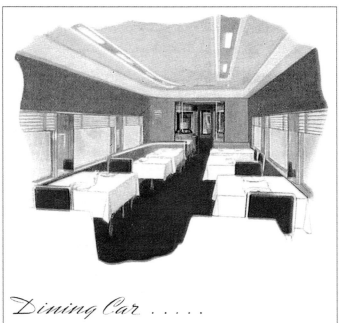

Dining Car . . . . .

A Section of the Dining Car

a few open sections—one in each 17-roomette *City*-series car—though not for sale. In the center of the car, where roomette 9 would have been, was a lengthwise extension sofa and an upper berth, presumably for the car's porter. Apparently, although roomette berths were designed to be pulled down by the passengers themselves, some still preferred assistance from the porter in making up their beds; for them, the sofa offered a place to wait while the porter worked.

Again the brochure: "The roomette is the most recent innovation in train sleeping quarters. Within the same space as the old section is now found an enchanting private room, procurable at section cost. Tasteful, livable and spacious, it includes disappearing toilet facilities, clothes lockers, adjustable footrest, and in-a-wall bed." Because this concept was so new, NYC had, for two weeks the previous August and September,

Forward Section of the Solarium

Solarium End of Observation Car

PULLMAN

MANHATTAN ISLAND

The *Island*-series observation lounges were no doubt the *Century*'s most famous cars. They contained sleeping space for only four: two in a double bedroom and two in a master room, the train's most luxurious accommodation. This left ample room for two generous lounge areas, one in the solarium end and one in the car's center section. In the exterior builder's photo below, note that the

tested on the *Century* a demonstrator roomette car from Pullman named *Roomette I*. (Pennsy tried out the car too, in August.)

The unfamiliarity of the roomettes—as well as their evolution from the open section—was clearly implicit in the somewhat clumsy description by a *New York Times* reporter covering a June 9 New York City–Albany test run of the new, streamlined *20th Century Limited* rolling stock. "What corresponds to the ordinary type of sleeping cars are equipped with sections from which the upper berths have been eliminated," he explained. "These sections are self-contained, with running water and other conveniences, and are furnished with sliding doors."

The four observation-lounges—*Bedloes Island*, continued on page 89

competition lurks: one of the PRR's "Fleet of Modernism" observation cars is poking its tail out behind *Manhattan Island*. The scarcity of revenue space aboard these *Island*-series cars put them in retirement during World War II. They returned to *Century* service in 1946, rebuilt as 4-double bedroom buffet-lounge observations. EXTERIOR: PULLMAN-STANDARD; THREE RENDERINGS, JOE WELSH COLLECTION

Lounge Section of Observation Car

RIGHT AND BELOW: *Wabash River* and its mates *Genesee River* and *Maumee River* were 1-compartment 1-drawing room 2-double bedroom buffet-lounge observations built in 1939 for the New York–St. Louis *Southwestern Limited*. During World War II, they replaced the revenue-capacity-shy *Island* cars on the *Century*, by government edict. The elegance of the solarium interior suggests that this exchange was not a major downgrading. The antenna on the roof is for the radio. EXTERIOR: T. S. MORTORANO, KEVIN J. HOLLAND COLLECTION; INTERIOR, PULLMAN–STANDARD

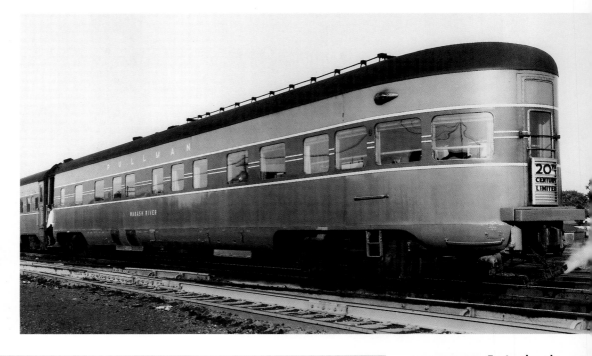

P.42307.
L.6567.
4-20-39. J.V.V
PLAN. A.4082.

FACING PAGE UPPER: Tearing through Manitou, N.Y., Class J3a 4-6-4 No. 5410—a 1937 product of the American Locomotive Company—has the honors of hauling the *Century* on this July 14, 1940. On occasions when one of the regularly assigned streamlined 4-6-4s was not available because of shopwork or a variance in operating situations, a regular Hudson (or 4-8-4 Niagara) pinch hit. THE EDWARD L. MAY MEMORIAL COLLECTION, COURTESY RICHARD L. STOVING

RIGHT: On June 15, 1948, as the westbound *Century* catches the late sun at Garrison, N. Y., observation *Pelee Island* is just months away from being upstaged by soon-to-be-delivered *Creek*-series cars; already diesels are up front. Directly ahead of the observation car is a transcontinental sleeper en route to Los Angeles, courtesy of the Santa Fe. The observation and the NYC Pullmans show a paint-scheme change made after the train's 1938 debut: narrowed aluminum window-band stripes; the blue stripes delineating the window band changed to aluminum; and the aluminum stripes at the top and bottom of the car sides eliminated. Compare with the cars in the top photo. ED NOWAK, NEW YORK CENTRAL, PETER V. TILP COLLECTION

continued from page 85

Manhattan Island, *Pelee Island*, and *Thousand Islands*—were no doubt the train's best-known cars, and the most starkly machine-age in ambiance. Here was Dreyfuss' cleanlining at its cleanest. The promotional literature called the main lounge section in the middle of the car a "stunning room with its narrow gun-metal columns and blue leather couches against captivating gray leather walls. Decorative lighting, novelty end murals, moveable pigskin chairs, walnut magazine tables, and a luxurious gray carpet emphasize the striking scheme of conservative modernism."

The solarium in the rounded observation end was decorated in tones of gray and pigskin and featured two rear-facing semicircular settees for panoramic viewing. A bulkhead separated the solarium from the main lounge. On the solarium side was a speedometer—*de rigeur* in the best observation cars—and, in two of the cars, pictorial maps of the New York Central System. The other two cars offered models of the train's normally assigned motive power—the J3a streamlined Hudson—displayed in glass-front cases.

Also in the observation car was the train's most luxurious accommodation: the master room. This swish space for two travelers had a pair of lower berths, four moveable club chairs, two windows, a shower, and a radio. A door opened into the adjacent double bedroom, yielding a suite.

The *New York Times* article suggested that the primary purpose of the test run of the new *Century* was "to demonstrate that steam remains supreme in railway transit"—a claim, *vis-a-vis* streamliners at least, that Santa Fe, Burlington, Union Pacific, Rock Island, and other roads that

Running along the Park Avenue Viaduct at 106th Street in Manhattan, No. 26 is just a few miles away from the bumping post at Grand Central Terminal, the end of its 16-hour journey from Chicago. It's October 1938, so the streamlined *Century* is nearly new. Shortly the tracks will plunge underground into the Park Avenue Tunnel, and real-estate values will soar as high-rise doorman buildings replace the low-rise tenements of Harlem seen here. The 660-volt DC third-rail electrification extends from GCT to Harmon, where T-motor 270 took over the *Century* from a J3a Hudson. ED NOWAK, NEW YORK CENTRAL, PETER V. TILP COLLECTION

had by this time introduced diesel-electric-powered trains would probably have disputed. But those Hudsons—developed under the direction of Paul W. Kiefer, chief engineer of motive power and rolling stock, and styled with great panache by Dreyfuss—were a remarkable blending of utility and beauty, of form and function. In an earlier trial they had been clocked at 123 miles per hour, and they did not lack power.

The ten streamlined Hudsons—Nos. 5445–5454—were a part of the subclass J3a, which totaled 50 locomotives, all built by Alco in 1937 and 1938. They were truly splendid in light gray livery. Tenders carried the dark gray band and silver and blue striping that led directly into the horizontal design elements running the entire length of the train.

Dreyfuss had drawn up an alternative proposal for the locomotive and train livery, which was presented alongside the one that was chosen and eventually became so famous. In the alternative scheme, locomotive tender and train were a dark color, with a light window band, a scheme reminiscent of Dreyfuss' *Mercury*. That window band terminated in the middle of the mail-baggage car, rather than extending across the tender side as it would in the final scheme, and it ended in a semicircle, a design conceit used by Raymond Loewy in his Fleet of Modernism for PRR and other railroad work.

The inaugural run of the streamlined *20th Century* attracted considerable interest. Since it occurred on June 15, nearly the longest day of the year, there was long, lingering evening light to illuminate the new

continued on page 95

Who's Who on the "Century"

...calling the roll aboard the flagship
of New York Central's wartime fleet

Ticket Team
New York Central and Pullman Conductors collect tickets together. Yet that's the least of their jobs. Former is responsible for operation of the train, while the latter's exacting task is to make passengers as comfortable as possible under wartime conditions.

DORMITORY FOR CREW

"Key" Man in Wartime
With thousands of production executives riding the Century, the Secretary is a "key" man in more ways than one. He types many a war-important letter or document. And he registers passengers so as to reach them quickly if telegrams arrive en route.

Commissary Commander
Your Steward holds a difficult post. He strives to maintain standards of food and service despite rationing and the fact that many experienced cooks and waiters have changed their New York Central uniforms for Uncle Sam's.

The Press of War
Sudden errands of war often allow little time for packing, and may last longer than expected. So the services of the Valet on the 20th Century Limited in pressing and repairing clothes are particularly helpful in these hectic days.

Rear Guard Action
The Rear Brakeman is the train's "rear guard." Among his duties is checking with signal tower men, station agents and other railroaders along the route. They inspect each car as it speeds past, then signal a safety report to him.

Time for Dinner
Today, hundreds of busy executives count their meals en route among the few they have time and freedom to enjoy. Chefs, kitchen staffs and New York Central's Commissary Department do their utmost to see that those meals *are* enjoyed.

First Aid to First-Timers
War has brought many "first-timers" to the railroads. Porter shows each the air-conditioning regulator, reading lights, clothes closets, disappearing bed and toilette facilities, and other new comforts that foreshadow the "Trains of Tomorrow."

These are the men you *see*. But up ahead, the engineer and fireman handle your train with smooth efficiency. The baggage man and mail car crew care for their important cargoes. And all along the line are dispatchers, signalmen, track maintainers, shop workers and many others . . . each helping to man New York Central's fleet of some 800 passenger trains a day.

With fellow railroaders of America, they're learning new efficiencies from the wartime task of moving the greatest traffic in history. And tomorrow, they'll apply those lessons to bring you still finer travel aboard America's post-war trains.

New York Central's largest, most powerful, and most modern steam locomotives were the 4-8-4s that the railroad called "Niagaras." A fleet of 27 of these locomotives was built by Alco in 1945 and 1946. In June 1946 one of these husky Niagaras—a striking aesthetic contrast to the sleek streamlined J3a's—leads the *Century* out of Chicago's La Salle Street Station. A Rock Island commuter train, visible in the distance, is leaving at the same time. The heavyweight combine that leads the consist is a real anomaly. JOE COLLIAS, WILLIAM A. RAIA COLLECTION

We've got your *SLUMBER NUMBER* on the Water Level Route

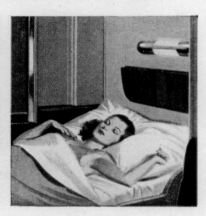

Is Climate your No. 1 slumber need?

For sound, refreshing sleep, do you like nights mild as spring or brisk as autumn? Choose your own ideal slumber climate. A twist of your wrist controls the temperature of the clean, fresh, conditioned air in your New York Central room.

Does Privacy rate first with you?

Your room has complete toilet facilities...so take your time preparing for bed or getting ready for breakfast. Your room assures quiet privacy...so turn in early if you wish...and take your fill, too, of early morning sleep.

Or is your Bed most important?

Do you need a roomy, perfectly-made bed...with downy pillows, soft sheets and fluffy blankets tucked in around a mattress that's like a lullaby itself? You get them all...plus the gentlest of trips on the smooth Water Level Route.

Coming! 30 New Dreamliners!

Central has ordered enough all-room sleeping cars for 30 new overnight *dreamliners!* Each has many *new* features, *plus* all the luxuries of the modern cars that now carry you swiftly, safely, with all-weather dependability over the *Water Level Route*.

NEW YORK CENTRAL

The Water Level Route
...You Can Sleep

continued from page 90

gray ghost all the way up the Hudson River to Albany and beyond. As the train sped west through the Mohawk Valley in the gathering dark, crowds continued to turn up at trackside. Even at Buffalo, reached at 12:25 A.M., a sizeable group was waiting on the platform to welcome the new train.

One of the passengers on that first run was Ward Allen Howe, who for decades wrote a column of railroad news for the *New York Times'* Sunday travel section. He filed this evocative, surprisingly comprehensive report:

"Impressions of the inaugural westbound run of the new *20th Century Limited*—speed . . . calmness of President Williamson at the starting ceremony . . . waving crowds along the way . . . view from observation end of all 13 cars as train rounds curve . . . flocks of inspectors and press agents . . . politeness of train personnel . . . quiet satisfaction of Designer Dreyfuss and Chief Engineer of Motive Power Kiefer . . . gliding smoothness of operation . . . the pile of rice in corridor outside a drawing room . . . Café Century and steak dinner . . . speedometer hand touching 85 . . . busy Train Secretary Smith . . . snugness of roomettes and their easy operation . . . luxury . . . speed."

This is a remarkably appealing kaleidoscope of images, ending with the two characteristics that most defined the *Century*—luxury and speed. But the 1938 edition of the streamliner would have what in retrospect seems a short career—just a few weeks more than a decade—before being replaced by a new streamliner. And for much of that time the exquisitely stylish train would run in the shadow of war.

LEFT: Surprisingly, this 1946 advertisement featuring a New York Central "gray fleet" train—the *Century* or possibly the *Commodore Vanderbilt*—shows the original 1938 paint scheme, which the railroad had begun phasing out by 1939. The war is over, and this ad looks ahead to the huge re-equipping program in the works: "Coming! 30 New Dreamliners!" The *Century* of 1948 will once again lead the fleet. KARL ZIMMERMANN COLLECTION

The *20th Century Limited* entered the diesel age in 1945, when Electro-Motive E7s began bumping the streamlined Hudsons off the train for which they were designed. Here E7A No. 4006 and E7B No. 4102, both delivered in October 1945 wearing a short-lived Dreyfuss-designed scheme that had a dark gray stripe against a light-gray carbody, lead the *Century* out of La Salle Street Station past a Rock Island steamer waiting with a commuter train. The fourth car back is the Los Angeles–New York Santa Fe sleeper. PETER V. TILP COLLECTION

5

THE FINAL FLOWERING

Though Henry Dreyfuss' 1938 *20th Century Limited* may have been a high-water mark in streamliner design, New York Central had one more impressive flourish to offer in presenting its flagship. This final *Century* would come in 1948, as part of a nationwide outpouring of re-equipped passenger trains that followed World War II—the American railroads' last, heroic, probably misguided attempt to impress and woo the rail traveler. Though it may have lacked the pure sophistication of the 1938 train, the 1948 edition—in which

Glowing in early morning sunlight dimmed by air made heavy from nearby steel mills, one of the *Creek*-series observation cars trails the westbound *20th Century Limited* making its station stop at Englewood on Chicago's South Side on a winter day in 1964. The train—the front of which is partially obscured by steam escaping from the train-heating system—is strung out around the curved platform that hugged the NYC main, the locomotives now facing north on the final leg of the trip into La Salle Street Station. JIM BOYD

97

Dreyfuss was again involved—had a lot to offer, including round-end observation cars that were among the most distinctive ever built. And the unique collection of amenities that characterized the *Century*—its all-Pullman, extra-fare status, its shower, barber, valet, and secretary—would remain.

The 1938 train's ten-year run, just a decade, by today's standards seems short. In spite of the war, the operations and appearance were little changed over those years. Even in the face of wartime austerity, Central kept the standards high aboard its flagship. (One compromise, and a slight one, had been to lay up the *Island*-series observation cars. With just one double bedroom and a master room, the cars were too shy of revenue space to pass muster with the Office of Defense Transportation, so they were

To publicize the 1948 re-equipping of its flagship, NYC issued this impressive *Book of the Century*, with die-cut cover (and the stacked-bar designwork in red flocking) and artist's impressions of the new train. Both the exterior and interior of the *Creek*-series observation's Lookout Lounge were deemed worthy of illustration. In addition to the lounge in the observation car, the 1948

Through Your Eyes ...

The following pages take you on an overnight vacation aboard the world's most famous train ... an overnight vacation between New York and Chicago, as seen through *your* eyes. It begins as you follow your own shadow down the crimson carpeted platform of Grand Central Terminal. For there ahead waits the 20TH CENTURY LIMITED...with its lighted insignia and the wide windows of its "Lookout Lounge" gleaming a soft welcome.

Refreshments at Twilight

From the depths of your Observation Car club chair, you find the atmosphere subtly relaxing. There's the sense of quiet sociability around you, as you sip refreshments before dinner, and drink in the twilit beauty rolling past outside. If you'd like a particularly fine view, two steps lead up to the CENTURY's raised "Lookout Lounge" . . . with its huge windows made to order for sightseeing along the Water Level Route.

replaced by *Genesee River*, *Maumee River*, and *Wabash River*, 1-compartment 1-drawing room 2-double bedroom buffet-lounge-observations built by P-S in 1939 for the *Southwestern Limited*.) *Century* timings were not radically effected by World War II, though in December 1942 the schedule was lengthened by one hour in both directions, to a still very impressive 17 hours. In April 1946 it was reduced once again to 16, and a year later the eastbound schedule was further trimmed to 15½ hours, the fastest timing ever.

In spite of the rigors of wartime service, which had left them cosmetically worn and in serious need of renewal, the 1938 *Century* cars still had plenty of good miles in them and were thus refurbished to become the core of *Century* running-mate *Commodore Vanderbilt*—a posh all-Pullman train on the New York–Chicago route that would have been almost any other railroad's flagship. In addition, some of the refurbished cars returned to serve on the *Century* itself. The splendid *Island*-series observations, for instance, returned to the *Century* in 1946, rebuilt as slightly less grand 4-double bedroom buffet-lounge-observations. They later appeared when needed on second sections of the 1948 *Century*. In fact, when the new *Century* was inaugurated on September 15, 1948, many of the sleepers were veteran cars, refurbished, repainted, and standing in admirably until the remaining cars of New York Central's massive postwar passenger-car order—an astonishing 742 cars all told—were delivered.

Century featured a mid-train lounge, the Century Club, which for the first time has migrated from the head end, where similar facilities had been located aboard the wooden-car, heavyweight, and first streamlined versions of the train. The radio telephone, available only from Buffalo east, is a new feature. Train secretary, barber, and shower are all *Century* traditions. WILLIAM F. HOWES JR. COLLECTION

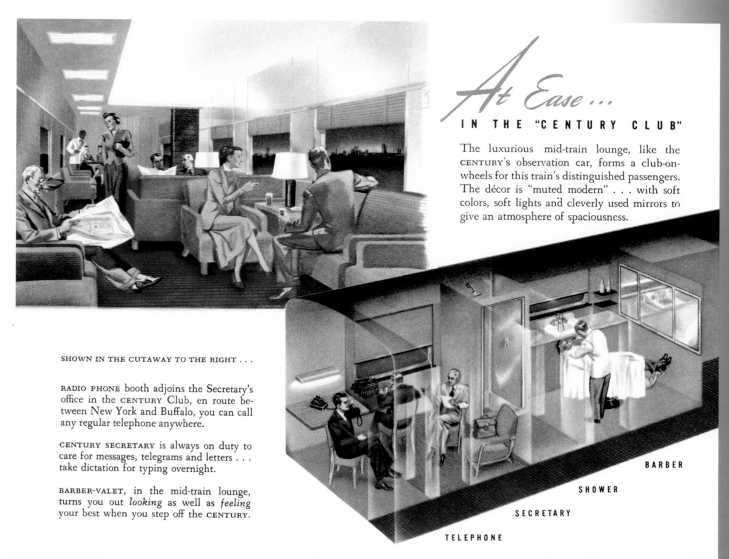

At Ease . . .
IN THE "CENTURY CLUB"

The luxurious mid-train lounge, like the CENTURY's observation car, forms a club-on-wheels for this train's distinguished passengers. The décor is "muted modern" . . . with soft colors, soft lights and cleverly used mirrors to give an atmosphere of spaciousness.

SHOWN IN THE CUTAWAY TO THE RIGHT . . .

RADIO PHONE booth adjoins the Secretary's office in the CENTURY Club, en route between New York and Buffalo, you can call any regular telephone anywhere.

CENTURY SECRETARY is always on duty to care for messages, telegrams and letters . . . take dictation for typing overnight.

BARBER-VALET, in the mid-train lounge, turns you out *looking* as well as *feeling* your best when you step off the CENTURY.

BARBER

SHOWER

SECRETARY

TELEPHONE

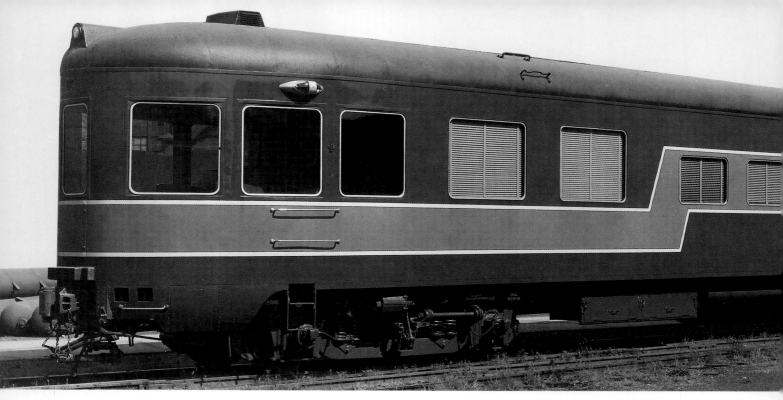

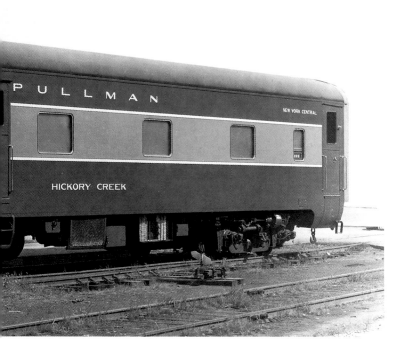

For this postwar *Century*, Central turned once again to Pullman-Standard for equipment, though by then it had begun to do business with the Edward G. Budd Manufacturing Company (after 1946, the Budd Company). Budd was P-S's major competitor in the lightweight era and arguably the most successful of all builders of streamliners. In fact, Budd had made a proposal to New York Central for the 1938 train—to no avail, though shortly thereafter it would win the contract for the flashy streamlined version of the New York–Buffalo *Empire State Express*, which had the bad luck to be inaugurated on December 7, 1941, as Pearl Harbor was attacked.

Although Budd would be the builder of much postwar equipment for NYC—the entirety of illustrious trains including the Chicago–Boston *New England States* (1949) and the coaches-only New York–Chicago *Pacemaker* (1948), plus important pieces of others—Pullman-Standard again got the nod for the *20th Century Limited*. Though relatively little of significance had changed in passenger-car design and amenities in war-distracted America from the mid-1930s to mid-1940s, Central was determined that its 1948 *Century* would be new enough to justify the hoopla with which the railroad planned to launch it. The events included a christening by noted actress Beatrice Lillie, with General Dwight D. Eisenhower (then president of Columbia University) participating in the ceremony.

The newness involved a modified paint scheme (a further evolution of the 1938 Dreyfuss dress) and dramatic new feature cars. Certainly the most memorable of these were the 5-double bedroom-buffet-lounge-observations *Hickory Creek* and *Sandy Creek*. What made these cars so special was their much-touted "Lookout Lounges." Trade magazine *Railway Age* described them this way: "In the observation end with raised floor level and extra-high windows, a light-green ceiling increases the effect of spaciousness. At the very end, facing the rear, is a sofa for two, upholstered in bright red leather. Forward of this section are four gun-metal, leather-covered chairs, then two sofas upholstered in a soft, gray-beige fabric, each seating three passengers, with a low coffee table between them."

Two somewhat oddly placed built-in, bright-red leather seats flanked the two steps leading down from the observation end to a small cocktail lounge, which had windows of traditional size. A small service bar, five double bedrooms, and the porter's section completed the floor plan of the *Creek* cars.

"Refreshments at Twilight," bannered the spread describing the *Creek* cars in Central's pre-inaugural publicity booklet. "From the depths of your Observation Car club chair, you find the atmosphere subtly relaxing," it read. "There's a sense of quiet sociability around you, as you sip refreshments before dinner, and drink in the twilit beauty rolling past outside. If you'd like a particularly fine view, two steps lead up to the *Century*'s raised 'Lookout Lounge,' with its huge windows made to order for sightseeing along the Water Level Route."

ABOVE: *Hickory Creek* (shown here in a builder's photograph made on August 30, 1948, just weeks before the re-equipped train's inaugural) and *Sandy Creek*, notable for the tall windows in the Lookout Lounge area, were among the finest observation cars ever built. PULLMAN-STANDARD, PETER V. TILP COLLECTION

LEFT: This view looking forward from the rounded end of the Lookout Lounge shows a *Creek* car in its as-built configuration. The painting on the bulkhead depicts ice being cut—a winter ritual that was routine in much of New York Central's territory in the era before electric refrigeration. Behind that wall lurks a small service buffet. Judging from the third-rail trackage visible through the windows, this publicity photo was taken during the car's layover at New York's Mott Haven Yard. PHIL AND BEV BIRK COLLECTION

The tall rear windows and raised observation area of the *Creek* cars are close to being unique. Three additional NYC cars—*Singing Brook, Sunrise Brook, Wingate Brook,* 5-double bedroom buffet-observation-lounges built in 1949 by Budd for the *Southwestern Limited*—also had Lookout Lounges with similarly high windows and step-ups. (*Sunrise Brook* and *Wingate Brook* often would be used as fill-in cars on the *Century* in the 1960s.) Eight *Royal*-series 5-double bedroom buffet-observation-lounges built by Pullman-Standard in 1950 for Southern Railway's *Crescent* and *Royal Palm* also had step-ups like the *Creek* cars.

In addition to *Hickory Creek* and *Sandy Creek*, the 1948 *Century's* feature cars were twin-unit diners and mid-train lounges *Lake Shore* and *Atlantic Shore,* which contained a barbershop, shower, secretary's room, and telephone booth. These cars maintained the Century Club tradition of style and elegance, with lounge areas comfortably arrayed with sofas and commodious club chairs in a manner that successfully evoked the atmosphere of an exclusive private men's or women's club in New York or Chicago, where there were plenty of each.

The diners also broke new ground for the *Century.* Although the 1938 train typically carried two traditional diners run back-to-back, the 1948 version featured twin-unit diner-kitchen-car pairs, with the kitchen car also providing dormitory space for the crew. Initially seating 68 (before a pair of tables was removed to provide space for passengers waiting to be seated by the steward), these cars were stylish and impressive in scope. Like their predecessors in *20th Century Limited* service, they would be laid with snowy linen, set with fine hotel-grade silver, and adorned with fresh flowers. Breaking up the long tunnel of space was a variation in seating arrangements—inward-facing double banquettes, for instance—and stylish partitions tricked out in broad horizontal striping of alternating silver-gray and maroon, the characteristic image created by Dreyfuss for the 1938 train.

Actually, P-S delivered four identical table cars to NYC. The additional two were paired with kitchen-lounge cars and when ordered had been intended for the second section of the *Century.* They were actually put into service on the *Commodore Vanderbilt,* another consist that lacked a *Shore*-series Century Club lounge.

In addition to the feature cars, the 1948 train had some innovative characteristics. Toilets were enclosed in annexes in all rooms (except the one-person roomettes, of course). Doors between the cars opened pneumatically, with a light touch on the handle. "They stay open to let you pass, then close softly," according to the inaugural brochure. Lighting was all fluorescent—an "advanced" feature that half a century later seems less than aesthetically pleasing. Radio-telephone service was available

Lake Shore (shown below) and *Atlantic Shore* were the 1948 *Century's* mid-train lounges and home to the barber and train secretary. The shower and radio telephone were also located there. PULLMAN-STANDARD, PETER V. TILP COLLECTION

OVERLEAF: This splashy two-page advertisement from the *Saturday Evening Post* ran on the occasion of the *Century*'s inaugural. The message was clear, with the word "new" or its variations appearing no fewer than 14 times in the ad's headlines and copy. MIKE MC BRIDE COLLECTION

RIGHT: Postal cachets were printed for collectors on the occasion of the first run of the 1948 *Century*. The cancellation on this one indicates that it was carried aboard the Railway Post Office car of No. 25, the westbound *Century*, two days after the inaugural ceremony. The loss of mail contracts and consequent elimination of the RPOs in the 1960s was another major blow to passenger railroading in its declining years. C. W. NEWTON COLLECTION

from a booth in the Century Club mid-train lounge, though only east of Buffalo. (Telephone service before departure from Grand Central Terminal and La Salle Street Station had been a long-standing *Century* feature, going back to the heavyweight era.)

Electrically cooled ice water circulated ("Pure, ice-cold drinking water is on tap in every *20th Century Limited* room") and from a "house phone" in every car, porters could make dinner reservations for travelers, order their refreshments, or summon the train secretary. A public-address system stood ready in the Lookout Lounge, Century Club, and diner for announcements or paging.

continued on page 109

World Premiere

New – from its streamlined Diesel to its raised "Lookout Lounge"!

Today, an all-new *20th Century Limited* proudly paces the century for which it is named. And more than newness sets this apart from other trains . . . a quality of atmosphere.

It's the festive feel of the dinner hour in the spacious new diner. It's the club-like sociability you enjoy in the new "Lookout Lounge." It's a sense of being served with distinction.

You'll recognize that traditional *Century* atmosphere at once on this first and finest of New York Central's new all-private-room *Dreamliner* fleet.

New **Step up into the Lookout Lounge.** Sip refreshments . . . and drink in the twilight beauty of the *Water Level Route* through huge new sightseeing windows.

New **Be seated in world's finest Diner.** It's so spacious it needs a separate kitchen car. Smart designing gives each table a sense of privacy plus a perfect outlook.

New Retire to your 1948 private room on the 20th Century Limited

New **If you're in a party,** you'll like the way two *Century* bedrooms can be opened up into one extra-large room . . . made to order for business conferences or entertaining.

New **If you're a couple,** you'll enjoy this new *Century* room. Two deep-mattressed beds . . . big wardrobe . . . circulating ice water . . . and new, enclosed washing and toilet facilities.

New **If you're alone,** a *Century* roomette is a air-conditioned sitting room—or private office that you can transform in a moment to a luxurious bedroom or complete dressing room.

the New 20th *Century Limited*

Between the Heart of Chicago—and the Heart of New York

Vacation overnight aboard the new Century. Sleep well on the smooth, Water Level Route. Arrive fresh, with no business time lost.

NEW **NEW YORK CENTRAL** NEW YORK CENTRAL SYSTEM

The Water Level Route—You Can Sleep

New **Century Club.** In this swank mid-train lounge you'll find the barber-valet, and the Century Secretary.

New **Keep in Touch.** Radio phone connects you with any telephone anywhere, right from the speeding *Century.*

On September 9, 1948, less than a week before its inauguration, the new *Century* was sent out on the main line partly for the benefit of company photographer Ed Nowak. Here the train is posed on a curve at Garrison, N.Y. There are no passengers in the Lookout Lounge—just the photographer's tripod. This and earlier versions of the "lightning-stripe" paint scheme that adorned the noses of the EMD E7 (and later E8) diesels were the work of designer Henry Dreyfuss. ED NOWAK, NEW YORK CENTRAL, PETER V. TILP COLLECTION

E7 diesels in impeccable dress gleam in the afternoon sun as they await departure from La Salle Street Station with No. 26 in 1948. HERBERT H. HARWOOD SR., HERBERT H. HARWOOD JR. COLLECTION

continued from page 103

Largely invisible to passengers were up-to-date technical details that the *Century* shared with other trains in the Great Steel Fleet—as well as the best trains operated by the competition. A single set of 4,000-horse-power Electro-Motive E7 diesels made the entire 961-mile run between New York and Chicago, a far cry from the multiple locomotive changes of the steam era. "Tight-lock couplers, cushioned in rubber, make the entire *Century* one unit for gliding-smooth starts and stops," according to the brochure. "The brakes are electro-pneumatic . . . pressure on all 160 wheels is automatically balanced for smooth, fast, safe stops. Springs combine coil and leaf types, with stabilizers to make New York Central's famous Water Level Route smoother still." Safety-glass windows were double-glazed and glare-proof.

A modified color scheme adorned the cars as well as the E7 diesel locomotives that had displaced Dreyfuss' elegant streamlined J3a Hudsons (and the businesslike Niagara 4-8-4s that sometimes hauled the *Century* when consists were heavy). This dress—white-lined light gray window band on darker gray body—is really a simplified, flip-flopped version of the earlier Dreyfuss scheme, sans the blue edging and silver stripes. Some of the earliest E7s carried a scheme to match the 1938 train, which they hauled at the end of its career. Later E7s, painted to match the 1948 train, carried a significantly different version of New York Central's famous "lightning-stripe" motif on their bulldog noses.

The Central had long touted its "Water Level Route," a relatively smooth, low-grade passage across the Eastern U.S. that insinuated itself along the banks of major waterways. (This stood in stark contrast to the Pennsylvania Railroad's route across its namesake state, which included a backbreaking hurdle over the Allegheny Mountains that required no less an engineering feat than the Horseshoe Curve to accomplish.) In introducing its "New *20th Century Limited*, Flagship of New York Central's Great Steel Fleet," the railroad played on this asset in a few ways. For one thing, the bottle that Bea Lillie smashed over *Hickory Creek*'s coupler contained the commingled waters of the Hudson River, Mohawk River, Lake Erie, and Lake Michigan, with all of which the *Century* was intimately acquainted.

The other nod came in car naming. All *Century* cars had water-connected names, recognizing the rivers, bays, ports, shores, islands, bridges, harbors, and creeks primarily (but not always) in Central territory. In addition to *Hickory Creek*, *Sandy Creek*, *Lake Shore*, *Atlantic Shore*, and the refurbished *Bedloes Island*, *Manhattan Island*, and *Thousand Islands*, there were *River*-series 10-roomette 6-double bedroom cars (*Hudson River*, *East River*, *Chicago River*), *Bay*-series 22-roomette cars (*Haverstraw Bay*, *Sandusky Bay*), and *Port*-series 12-double bedroom cars (*Port of Buffalo*, *Port of New York*, *Port of Chicago*). In keeping with the program, in 1949 the 14 *Imperial*-series 4-compartment 2-drawing room 4-double bedroom sleepers built for the 1938 *Century* were refurbished and renamed into the *Bridge* series (*Bear Mountain Bridge*, *George Washington Bridge*, *Rip Van Winkle Bridge*) for the new train. Budd-built *Harbor*-series 22-roomette cars (*Boston Harbor*, *Cleveland Harbor*) got into the act later, either as originally configured or rebuilt as Sleepercoaches.

The price tag from Pullman-Standard and the Electro-Motive Division of General Motors exceeded $4 million, a significant amount of money in the late 1940s. It was part of the huge investment in new passenger equipment made by the nation's passenger railroads immediately after World War II, an investment that most would agree went sour, and that few railroads would recoup.

NYC had led this charge into the hoped-for new era of revitalized passenger railroading. It was, in fact, a renewal that they'd been projecting long before the war had ended. Before the close of 1943, the railroad was making plans to continue the fleet renewal that had begun with the

The new feature cars ordered for the 1948 *Century*—just two of each—provided for only a single consist in each direction. Second sections were still run occasionally, however, filled out with equipment from the train's earlier incarnation. Here, on February 2, 1950, two sections of No. 25 have arrived at La Salle Street Station. A 1948 *Creek* observation is to the left and a 1938 *Island* car to the right. ED NOWAK, NEW YORK CENTRAL, PETER V. TILP COLLECTION

ABOVE: Its journey almost at an end, No. 26 has just crossed the Harlem River and is curving onto the Park Avenue Viaduct as S1 No. 100 pulls the consist of an earlier arrival at Grand Central Terminal out to Mott Haven Yard for servicing. The date is October 9, 1951, and heavyweight cars still routinely run in mixed consists with lightweights. The train on the far left track is a suburban run. The first of its class, electric "motor" No. 100 was built in 1904. Thirty-four sister locomotives would follow before production ended in 1909; the 100 has been preserved. Mott Haven is some five miles from Grand Central Terminal. ED NOWAK, NEW YORK CENTRAL, PETER V. TILP COLLECTION

1938 *Century* and 1941 *Empire State Express*. Passenger surveys probed at tastes and needs. What trains, running where, with what equipment, services, and amenities would find favor with the traveling public?

First came the "Post-War Railroad Coach Study," which helped the Central plan day trains. Then, in August 1944, a sleeping-car survey was conducted under the direction of Foote, Cone & Belding by the staff of Stewart, Brown & Associates. This "Survey of Passenger Preferences and Attitudes Concerning Post-War Design and Services for Sleeping Car Travel" was conducted by "trained women interviewers" who rode all the principal Central trains and handed questionnaires to passengers in "all types of sleeping accommodations." In all, 2,529 passengers were polled aboard the *20th Century Limited, Commodore Vanderbilt, Advance Commodore Vanderbilt, Detroiter, Ohio State Limited, Southwestern Limited, New England States, Lake Shore Limited*, and *Iroquois*. Sixty-seven percent of responding passengers were men, probably a reasonably accurate reflection of the ridership as a whole.

Interestingly, 62 percent of the men and only 31 percent of the women had taken an "airline trip on a regularly scheduled flight." When asked their preferred method of travel, men were almost exactly split between sleeping car (43.2 percent) and airplane (43.4 percent). On the other hand, women still clearly favored sleeping car (45.7 percent) over airplane (29.5 percent). About six percent of men preferred to travel by automobile, compared with 12 percent of women.

"The questionnaire covered all aspects of sleeping-car travel but concentrated primarily on facilities and services with which the passengers would be immediately familiar," according to the report's preamble. Seventy-seven percent of passengers reported that they used the club or lounge cars. Of these, 46 percent said they preferred the observation car, 37 percent the club car, while the balance had no preference. When asked about the location of the club lounge car, 47 percent preferred the center of the train, 23 percent the rear, and just one percent the front, while the balance had no preference or didn't answer. This was dramatic evidence that the traditional "combo" baggage-smoking lounge at the front of the train, a staple from the *Century's* inauguration right through the 1938 streamliner, was out of favor. It would not be replicated on the postwar trains.

Another dinosaur was the open section, which consistently lost out to roomettes and bedrooms. With the duplex roomette (with rooms staggered up and down, allowing more to fit in the same space) thrown into the mix, 47 percent preferred a roomette as a single accommodation, 26 percent a duplex roomette, and only seven percent a lower berth.

LEFT: In this late August view from 1954, work on a new bridge over the Harlem River proceeds in the foreground. The T-motor is pulling No. 25 from Mott Haven Yard into Grand Central Terminal for its evening departure. Once in the terminal area, the motor will run around its train and push the observation car up to the bumping post. Though it was acceptable for a switcher to pull other trains directly into GCT and then simply uncouple and remain trapped behind them until departure, this would never do for the *Century*. Whether open-platform or round-end, the observation car was the first thing a boarding passenger was to see. JOHN DZIOBKO

It's 1961 in Grand Central Terminal, and the gate sign for the *20th Century Limited* being cranked into place gives clues to the status of the flagship at that time. Now running combined with the *Commodore Vanderbilt/Pacemaker*, No. 25 made stops—Elkhart, South Bend, and Gary—it never had before. The train carried two Sleepercoaches (loading numbers SC23 and SC25) and, just ahead of them and behind the coaches (numbers not visible at the top of the photograph), a grill diner, less expensive than the regular diner and catering to the coach/Sleepercoach trade. DON WOOD

With these results in hand to help, Central management began to make decisions about what passenger service would be like, and before long the railroad's effective publicity machine was at work, promising a bright future for passengers along the New York Central System's far-flung lines.

Initial planning ran heavily to daytime services, and in the first half of 1944, orders were placed with Budd, Pullman-Standard, and American Car & Foundry for 300 cars, mostly day coaches, but also some diners, lounges, and observation cars. These provisional orders were finally executed when the war ended. Then, in December 1945, NYC ordered an additional 420 cars, many of them sleepers, said to be the largest single order for passenger cars ever, anywhere. This order was also shared by P-S (200 cars), Budd (112 cars), and ACF (108 cars). The price tag for the entire 720-car splurge: $58.9 million. At a time when the nation's railroads were falling all over each other in eagerness to bring passenger trains back up to snuff, New York Central was first among equals in this outpouring of optimism and enthusiasm. All the major carbuilders were flooded with orders that postwar material shortages made difficult for them to fill in a timely fashion. In fact, cars from NYC's 1944 and 1945 orders kept trickling in right up into 1950.

By 1946, however, Central was running enticing ads: "Coming! 30 New Dreamliners! Central has ordered enough all-room sleeping cars for 30 new overnight dreamliners! Each has many new features, plus all the luxuries of the modern cars that now carry you swiftly, safely, with all-weather dependability over the Water Level Route."

RIGHT AND BELOW: With the *Century* awaiting departure from GCT, cocktail hour has begun in the Lookout Lounge. It's 1961, and the *Creek* observations have been refurbished with reconfigured seating as part of the upgrading accorded Nos. 25 and 26 for their 60th birthday, coming the following year. The twin-unit diners with Century Club lounges were refurbished as well, and amenities such as corsages for the women and boutonnières for the men became standard. DON WOOD

And the 1948 *Century* was a "dreamliner" indeed, and in its first years of reign over a mid-century America, the train's luster was undimmed. This was the era of the much-remarked "Gold Dust Twins"—stewards Tommy O'Grady and Tommy Walsh, who held sway in the twin-unit diners, catering to and recalling the preferences of the rich and famous who, for a short time at least, would continue to patronize the train. These gregarious, loquacious Irishmen helped write another chapter highlighting *Century* celebrity, so much a characteristic of the train for more than 50 years.

Menu

NEW YORK CENTRAL SYSTEM

THE 20th CE

A La Carte

Bisque of Crab Cardinal, Cup 40; Tureen 55

Consomme Pointoise, Cup 40

Canapes of Imported Caviar (Beluga) 1.50

Chilled Honeydew with Lime 50

Tomato Juice 40

Fresh Shrimp Cocktail Lorenzo 1.00

Golden Omelette with Julienne of Canadian Bacon or Stewed Fresh Tomatoes, Garden Vegetable, Persillade Potatoes 2.15

Home Style Roast Beef Hash, Pickle Chips, Buttered Zucchini, Bowl of Salad 2.30

Fresh Shrimp and King Crab Meat Salad, Hard Boiled Egg, Sliced Tomatoes, Saratoga Chips 2.65

Charcoal Broiled Half Chicken, Hunter Style, Minted Green Peas, Baked Stuffed Potato 3.20

Club Sandwich, 20th Century 2.00

Grilled Imported Sardines on Toasted Rye Bread, Tomato Salad 1.50

Combination Salad 85

The Salad Bowl with Ry-Krisp 1.10

Lettuce and Tomato Salad 80

Pineapple Salad, French Dressing 1.00

Old Fashioned Peach Shortcake, Whipped Cream 55

N.Y.C. Special Ice Cream 45

Dark Pitted Sweet Cherries, Cookies 45

Butterscotch Sundae 55

Coconut Pudding, Fruit Sauce 50

Chilled Melon 50

Imported Roquefort, Liederkranz or Gruyere Cheese, Crackers or Ry-Krisp 50

Coffee, Pot 40	Malted Milk, Pot 30	Individual Milk 25
Tea, Pot 30	Instant Coffee, Pot 35	Cocoa, Pot 30
Sanka, Pot 35	Postum, Pot 35	Iced Tea 35	Iced Coffee 40

Please write on check each item desired.   Waiter cannot accept verbal orders.

A charge of 50 cents per person will be made for meals served in rooms.

Your comments and suggestions about any aspect of our dining service will be sincerely appreciated.

Please address:

A. H. SMITH, Manager Dining Service, 260 East 161st Street, New York 51, N. Y.

25-26-D

8-26
9-15-54

When the *20th Century Limited* did finally lose its luster—and that happened in the decade after its final re-equipping—it was largely because of widespread, seemingly inexorable trends in the travel patterns of Americans. In huge numbers, they were deserting trains for the independence granted by the automobile and the speed of airplanes. From 1946 to 1953, passenger losses quintupled for railroads nationwide. Certainly 1956 was a watershed year, as it saw Congress establishing the Highway Trust Fund and passing the Interstate Highway Act. The Defense Highway System was a pet project of President Dwight Eisenhower; there's some irony in the fact that, just eight years earlier, he had presided over the inauguration of the "New" *20th Century Limited*.

Along with these national political trends, internal politics at New York Central had a good deal to do with the deteriorating stature of the Great Steel Fleet as the 1950s wore on. A key and complex figure in this drama was Robert R. Young, industry gadfly and compulsive, vocal passenger-train supporter. As chairman of the board of Chesapeake & Ohio, he planned a total postwar renewal of that railroad's passenger operations and was responsible for a huge (given the relatively modest scope of that coal-hauling railroad's passenger operations) car order, 351 all told. The highlight of this rebirth was to be an all-new train: the ultra-luxury, daytime *Chessie*, which was to feature dome cars and an array of other amenities. Eventually, cooler heads prevailed, and—in an embarrassing reversal—the *Chessie* was scrubbed just before its inaugural (though after the train had been assembled for publicity photographs), and as many car orders were cancelled as could be. Only 130 cars were actually delivered to C&O.

Earlier, Young had made a big splash with his provocative magazine ads pointing out that pigs could cross the country without changing trains but that human passengers couldn't. In 1946 a group of Eastern and Western railroads, including NYC, began offering transcontinental through-sleeper service, an enterprise that was never hugely successful or profitable. The *20th Century* carried such sleepers for a time.

Young's interest in the Central began in the mid-1940s, about the time his passenger dreams for C&O were fading. With the Alleghany Corporation (which controlled the C&O and held stock in NYC) as his power base, Young launched into a prolonged, bitter, brutal, unprecedentedly public battle for control of the NYC with then-president William White. At the May 1954 stockholders' meeting, Young emerged victorious from a proxy fight, and one of the nation's proudest railroads (though far closer to insolvency than Young knew) was in his control.

As chairman of the railroad, Young remained as pro-passenger as ever, as the promise to further invigorate NYC passenger service with innovative thinking had been one of the arrows in his quiver in his battle with White. On the other hand, Alfred E. Perlman, the tough-minded, cold-hearted president Young brought with him, stood firmly in the other corner. Perlman had hauled the Denver & Rio Grande Western out of bankruptcy, in part by being ruthless in paring off appendages deemed outmoded and unprofitable: in the case of the D&RGW, many of its nar-

RY LIMITED

Dinner

| Ripe Olives | Spiced Melon Rind | Radishes Rosette |
| Celery Farcie | | Green Olives |

Bisque of Crab Cardinal	Chilled Honeydew with Lime
Consomme Pointoise	Tomato Juice
Canapes of Anchovies	Fresh Shrimp Cocktail Lorenzo 50c

FILET OF FRESH GASPE SALMON SAUTE, MEUNIERE, CUCUMBERS
Buttered Zucchini, Baked Stuffed Potato............ 4.00

ROAST LONG ISLAND DUCKLING, CELERY DRESSING, BIGARADE
Minted Green Peas, Persillade Potatoes............ 4.10

CALF'S LIVER ON CANADIAN BACON, 20TH CENTURY
with Button Mushrooms and Fines Herbes Sauce
Garden Vegetable, Potatoes Hashed Browned Lyonnaise............ 4.30

ROAST RIBS OF BEEF, NATURAL GRAVY
Cauliflower Polonaise, Potatoes du Jour............ 4.50

LAMB CHOPS GRILLE, PINEAPPLE GLACE
Minted Green Peas, Baked Stuffed Potato............ 4.50

CHARCOAL BROILED SELECTED SIRLOIN STEAK
(Button Mushrooms included on request)
Buttered Zucchini, Potatoes Hashed Browned Lyonnaise............ 5.85

Lettuce and Tomato Salad, Thousand Island Dressing

Old Fashioned Peach Shortcake, Whipped Cream	Butterscotch Sundae
N.Y.C. Special Ice Cream	Dark Pitted Sweet Cherries, Cookies
Chilled Melon	Coconut Pudding, Fruit Sauce
Gruyere, Liederkranz or Imported Roquefort Cheese, Ry-Krisp or Crackers	

| Coffee, Hot or Iced | Individual Milk | Tea, Hot or Iced |

This *Century* menu from September 1954 reflects rail dining at its best—the finest ingredients, prepared in attractive but essentially straightforward ways. Recipes changed to reflect changing tastes, but that formula served the Central's flagship well throughout its six and a half decades of service. The option of ordering either a complete dinner or à la carte was standard.
WILLIAM F. HOWES JR. COLLECTION

row-gauge branches had to go. If Young believed in improving passenger service, Perlman would have been just as happy to eliminate it. Initially, Perlman stayed the course, waiting, while Young experimented unsuccessfully with lightweight trains such the *Aerotrain* and *The Xplorer*.

NYC's income statements better supported Perlman's approach than they did Young's. Between 1948 and 1954, passenger revenues dropped from $136.5 million to $106.5 million. In the next decade, they plummeted to under $55 million. During this period, however, service curtailments were rampant, so losses did not escalate as quickly as revenues dropped.

While various members of the Great Steel Fleet were laid up, combined, or downgraded, the flagship sailed proudly on, above the fray. But services were interrelated, and in time the strong were pulled down with the weak. And when, in January 1958, a personal tragedy struck the Central and Robert Young committed suicide, NYC passenger trains lost their shield.

In the early, optimistic postwar years when the railroad's "30 all-new overnight Dreamliners" were fresh from the builders, car dispatchers were scrupulous in maintaining the particular cosmetic flavor of the best trains. The *Century*, the *Commodore Vanderbilt*, the *Detroiter* would inevitably travel with matched consists of Pullman-Standard cars tricked out in two tones of gray. Conversely, the *New England States*, the *Empire State Express*, the *Pacemaker*, and the *Southwestern Limited* were stainless-steel trains built largely by Budd. In time this nicety was lost, however, at first for convenience's sake, later because of train combinations.

One of the first of such combinations of New York–Chicago trains had occurred when the coaches-only *Pacemaker* and the all-Pullman *Commodore Vanderbilt* were merged, though they continued to be listed separately in the public timetables. These combinations and downgradings did not reach the *Century* until April 27, 1958, just a few months after Young's death, when the unthinkable happened: Through combination with the *Commodore Vanderbilt* (which by then was carrying coaches, by virtue of the *Pacemaker* name, of course), the *20th Century Limited* lost most of the characteristics that had lent it distinction since 1902.

It was no longer all-Pullman. Its extra fare accordingly was dropped, and stops were added. The *Century* never had been a train catering to "shorts"—passengers traveling between relatively local city pairs, such as South Bend and Toledo—but rather was restricted to through business. When the 1938 streamliner was inaugurated, for example, it stopped westbound only at Harmon, Albany, Syracuse, and Buffalo to pick up passengers and at Englewood only to drop. Eastbound pick-up stops were Englewood and Toledo with drops only at Albany and Harmon.

In addition to the added stops, the *Century*'s wonderful Century Club lounges, *Lake Shore* and *Atlantic Shore*, were withdrawn. (They were sold the following year to the Rock Island. The bulk of the railroad's pre-war streamlined cars were sold during this period as well, as were the 1948 P-S 22-roomette cars; the majority of all these went to Canada or Mexico.) Another watershed event for the *Century* in

BELOW: A worker at Budd's Red Lion, Pa., plant puts the symbolic finishing touches on the lettering of one of four 24-single room 8-double room Sleepercoaches leased to NYC by the carbuilder. These budget sleepers, which entered service on the *Century* and Boston–Chicago *New England States* in October 1959, brought private rooms to Central travelers at very modest cost: just regular coach fare plus $7 for a single room or $12.60 for a double. "Each Sleepercoach room offers complete privacy," according to a brochure touting the new service, "with a comfortable armchair, large picture window, private toilet facilities, mirror and baggage space, and a comfortable bed. There are double rooms for persons traveling together, and cribs are available for mothers with infants." LAWRENCE S. WILLIAMS, THE BUDD COMPANY, PHIL AND BEV BIRK COLLECTION

This brochure promoting Central's Sleepercoaches shows one of the ten 16-single room 10-double room cars rebuilt by the Budd Company from NYC's 22-roomette *Harbor*-series sleepers in 1961. In addition to the *Century*, the *New England States*, *Wolverine*, and other trains carried these budget cars. MIKE SCHAFER COLLECTION

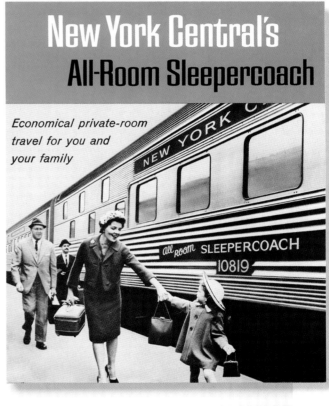

New York Central's All-Room Sleepercoach

Economical private-room travel for you and your family

1958 was the dropping of the Pullman contract, ending a relationship that had existed since 1902, when the train was born.

Suddenly, with all these changes made to the Central's flagship, the Pennsy's *Broadway Limited* emerged from the shadow of the *20th Century*, where it had long labored. Pennsy now touted it as the only all-Pullman train between New York and Chicago (though it had dropped its extra fare 16 years earlier), and some *Century* patrons did indeed head for Pennsylvania Station instead of Grand Central or Union instead of La Salle Street.

One last expression of the *20th Century Limited*'s affinity for glamour, celebrity, and movie stardom came with Metro-Goldwyn-Mayer's release in 1959 of *North by Northwest*, a comedy-thriller directed by Alfred Hitchcock. In this film, Roger Thornhill (played by Cary Grant) is an advertising executive who is mistaken for a spy, setting off a cross-country chase that culminates on Mount Rushmore, with Thornhill and his pursuers climbing across the presidents' faces. Since there is "no place to hide on a plane," Thornhill sneaks aboard the *Century* at Grand Central (in scenes filmed on location) for the run to Chicago. Once aboard he meets Eve Kendall (Eva Marie Saint). Hitchcock was a stickler for detail, and the *Century* scenes are as authentic as they come. The correct train number (25) is heard being called out by the train announcer in the Grand Central scenes; Grant walks down the platforms past the Pullmans that were indeed assigned to the the 1948 train. Scenes of mutual seduction shot in the diner (using both actual interiors and sound-stage interiors modeled after *Century* diners) correctly included the Hudson River outside the window, with *20th Century Limited* menus in full view. The scenes of Thornhill and Kendall in her drawing room are both quintessentially romantic and evocative of the lingering magic of train travel. Arrival at Chicago was filmed on location at La Salle Street Station.

In reality as well as in celluloid, the *20th Century Limited* did have one last surge of excellence, though it never shed the Budd-built *Pacemaker* coaches that had infiltrated the consist. In 1961 the process began, with remodeling and refurbishment of the twin-unit diners with a lounge and the wonderful *Creek*-series observation cars. A modest "Welcome Aboard" folder prepared in 1962 boasts "Luxury service at no extra cost. You are on one of the world's most famous trains . . . a train whose name has always been synonymous with luxurious travel." Inside, it points out that "The *20th Century Limited* is known for three things—dependability of its schedule, the tasteful elegance of its appointments, and the variety of special services it offers to make your trip comfortable, convenient and completely enjoyable."

An Electro-Motive E7 booster (cabless) locomotive sandwiched between E8 cabs launches a lengthy *Century* on its overnight journey from Chicago to New York City on a summer afternoon in 1962. The Budd section of the train—coaches and grill diner, with Sleepercoach presumably hidden around the bend—dominates this view taken from the Roosevelt Road overpass just south of Chicago's Loop. To the rear would be the Pullman-Standard equipment: sleepers, twin-unit diner, and observation car. The final lightning-stripe paint scheme is in its full glory—but it's also in its twilight years. By this time, the new, simplified "cigar-band" locomotive paint scheme had been introduced on some locomotives. GEORGE SPEIR

The folder goes on to itemize these services: dinner and breakfast in the Century Room, with complimentary champagne or sparkling burgundy and "corsages for the ladies, and at breakfast boutonniéres for the gentlemen." In the mid-train lounge and Lookout Lounge, along with magazines and refreshments, the *Hotel Red Book*, *Official Railway Guide*, and stationery were available. "You will enjoy complimentary hors d'oeuvres served in the lounge cars before dinner." Your porter would shine your shoes if you left them in the shoebox overnight, arrange valet service if your clothes were rumpled, get you a Remington "25" electric shaver if you needed it, or even an Olivetti Underwood typewriter if you felt ambitious or creative. Morning papers would appear in the diner and lounges. And, for a buck a bag, luggage could be

By late summer 1966, the days are dwindling for the *Century*, but you'd never guess it from this view off the Roosevelt Road overpass of No. 26 leaving Chicago. Passengers are already comfortably ensconced in *Sandy Creek*, which still looks impeccable. GEORGE SPEIR

transferred at Chicago to no fewer than 15 connecting trains headed west.

The coaches remained, joined by a welcome new addition: the Sleepercoach, with budget sleeping accommodations. Chicago, Burlington & Quincy had pioneered this thrifty concept in the fall of 1956 as part of the re-equipping of the *Denver Zephyr*. Like the rest of the cars in these consists (the last completely new trains delivered in America in the pre-Amtrak era), these four cars—Burlington called them "Slumbercoaches"—were built by the Budd Company. Other Slumbercoach operators were Northern Pacific, Baltimore & Ohio, and Missouri Pacific.

New York Central's first four Sleepercoaches (each with 24 single rooms and eight double rooms) came on lease from Budd and entered service on the *Century* in the fall of 1959. Then, in 1961, NYC sent ten

continued on page 124

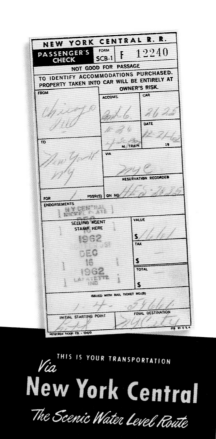

LEFT: This ticket allowed a lucky traveler to board the *20th Century Limited* in Chicago on December 21, 1962, and ride to New York City in roomette 6— arriving well in time to celebrate the Christmas holidays. The train was then in its final renaissance, upgraded for its 60th birthday, which it had celebrated just six months earlier. WILLIAM F. HOWES JR. COLLECTION

BELOW: As was often the case in the mid 1960s, *Wingate Brook*—Budd-built for the New York–St. Louis *Southwestern Limited*—is standing in for a *Creek* observation as No. 25 rolls past 16th Street tower on its last mile into La Salle Street Station in July 1965. The *Century* has just crossed the tracks of the St. Charles Air Line Company. MIKE SCHAFER

ABOVE: It's the mid 1960s, and the Electro-Motive E-units wear the Central's final, simplified paint scheme as they hustle the *Century* through the industrial landscape of northwest Indiana on a hazy summer late afternoon. JIM BOYD

RIGHT: On a placid summer evening along the Hudson River in 1962, No. 25 glides through Roa Hook, N.Y., with the Bear Mountain Bridge—a Hudson River landmark that has become almost symbolic of the *Century*'s riverside journey— just ahead. JOHN DZIOBKO

As the westbound *20th Century Limited* sweeps through Crugers, N.Y., on August 6, 1967, it still looks very much a going concern. The sands have nearly emptied through the hourglass for "The Greatest Train in the World," however. In less than four months it and the rest of the "Great Steel Fleet" will be gone. PETER V. TILP

Harbor-series 22-roomette cars to Budd for rebuilding as Sleepercoaches with 16 single rooms and ten doubles. In addition to the *Century*, these cars were used on the Boston–Chicago *New England States*, the New York–Cincinnati *Ohio State Limited*, the New York–Cleveland *Cleveland Limited*, and the New York–Chicago *Wolverine* and *Chicagoan*. (This attempt to make passenger service more viable was short-lived; by fall 1964, NYC would be selling four of these ten rebuilds to Northern Pacific.)

Still, the Central did try to maintain the standards aboard its flagship and hold onto the amenities reintroduced in 1961 and 1962. The

railroad remained fussy about assigning only the best cars to the train, for instance. As late as October 1966, the typical consist looked like this: a baggage-RPO built for the 1938 *Century*, followed by the Budd half of the train—a baggage-dorm, coach, grill diner, Sleepercoaches *York Harbor* and *South Haven Harbor* (both of them former 22-roomette cars), and 22-roomette sleeper *Ogdensburg Harbor*. To the rear was the Pullman-Standard section, all cars built in 1948–49: a lounge-kitchen and dining-room twin-unit pair, 12-bedroom sleepers *Port of Albany* and *Port of Boston*, and the incomparable 5-bedroom lounge-observation *Hickory Creek*. The red carpet was still rolled out every afternoon at Grand Central.

But ridership continued to wilt, and—as was the case with long-distance passenger service on most of the country's railroads—the days of the Great Steel Fleet were numbered. Still, the end came with great and cataclysmic suddenness, stunning in that it was unexpected. The prelude came on November 5, 1967, when the *New England States* was combined with the *Century* west of Buffalo. Then, only a few weeks later, on December 2, 1967, it abruptly ended: Making their last departure that day were not just the *20th Century Limited* but also the *Empire State Express*, *Ohio State Limited*, *Wolverine*, and other name trains across the system, replaced by anonymous trains shorn of amenities along with identities.

Attention in the press and among the faithful naturally focused on the *20th Century* (and, to add insult to injury, No. 25 was nine hours late into Chicago on its last run because of a freight-train derailment). Gone was the apt and famous name created by George Daniels. Gone the red carpet. Gone the wonderful observation car with the Lookout Lounge. You could still travel between New York and Chicago on a schedule approximating the *Century*'s, but it wasn't the same. Not by far.

In the early morning hours of December 3, 1967, comes a rainy post-midnight requiem for the *20th Century Limited* at Buffalo, as Nos. 25 and 26 pause there for the last time ever. Number 26, trailed by *Hickory Creek* (BELOW) would arrive at Grand Central Terminal in a timely fashion later that morning, but No. 25 with *Wingate Brook* (FACING PAGE) would not be so fortunate. Delayed by a freight derailment near Conneaut, Ohio, and ultimately detoured over the Norfolk & Western's former Nickel Plate main line, this train would not straggle into La Salle Street Station until 6:40 P.M., making it the very last of countless thousands of *Century*s to operate in the course of 65 illustrious years. EDWARD L. JOSCELYN, PETER V. TILP COLLECTION

6

THE GREAT STEEL FLEET

The *20th Century Limited* was extraordinary as a single train. Even more astonishing is the fact that, on the New York Central, it was just one among many members of an esteemed group of east-west long-distance trains known as the "Great Steel Fleet." The membership included many sections of the *Century* itself.

Throughout the heavyweight era, the *Century* routinely ran in multiple sections; some years the section count averaged more than three in each direction. For a few of those years, an *Advance 20th*

It's mid-morning at St. Louis, Mo., on August 4, 1966, as the westernmost member of New York Central's Great Steel Fleet, the *Southwestern*, exits Union Station. The once-esteemed liner is now down to a single sleeper and two coaches, plus a bevy of heavyweight head-end cars. At Indianapolis in late afternoon, the train will pick up a buffet-lounge car to serve beverages and light meals through the dinner hour. In late evening, the *Southwestern* will arrive at Cleveland; its buffet-lounge will turn back to St. Louis on the next morning's *Knickerbocker* while the sleeper and the coaches will be transferred to the *New England States* to be forwarded to Buffalo. There they will be switched to the New York-bound *Hendrick Hudson*. Such fragmented service represented the twilight years of Central's once-expansive fleet. MIKE SCHAFER

127

Century Limited had its own slot in the timecard. When the first streamlined *Century* was launched in 1938, enough equipment had been acquired from Pullman-Standard to field two daily sections in each direction. And though only two each of the "feature cars"—the *Creek*-series observations, the twin-unit diners, the *Shore*-series mid-train lounges—were built at the time of the 1948 re-equipping, second sections remained common, run with refurbished observation and lounge cars from the 1938 train.

But even in its multiple sections the *Century* was just the tip of the iceberg, the iceberg being the vast array of additional luxury trains that plied the far-flung New York Central Lines, later called the New York Central System. Many of these trains were running mates on the *Century's* New York–Chicago route via Cleveland and Toledo, or on the alternate Michigan Central route north of Lake Erie that linked those same end-points; others served different cities, notably those on the "Big Four"—the Cleveland, Cincinnati, Chicago & St. Louis Railway, a subsidiary of the New York Central like Michigan Central and Boston & Albany.

September 29, 1929, is an intriguing moment in time to

9 A Fleet of
TWENTY-HOUR TRAINS
in the NEW YORK-CHICAGO Service

◆

5 CHICAGO to NEW YORK

Fast Mail
Lv CHICAGO 9:50 AM   *Ar* NEW YORK 6:50 AM

The Wolverine
(via Michigan Central)
Lv CHICAGO 11:00 AM   *Ar* NEW YORK 8:00 AM

Advance 20th Century Limited
Lv CHICAGO 12:00 Noon   *Ar* NEW YORK 9:00 AM

20th Century Limited
Lv CHICAGO 12:40 PM   *Ar* NEW YORK 9:40 AM

The Commodore Vanderbilt
Lv CHICAGO 2:00 PM   *Ar* NEW YORK 11:00 AM

4 NEW YORK to CHICAGO

Advance 20th Century Limited
Lv NEW YORK 2:00 PM   *Ar* CHICAGO 9:00 AM

20th Century Limited
Lv NEW YORK 2:45 PM   *Ar* CHICAGO 9:45 AM

The Commodore Vanderbilt
Lv NEW YORK 4:00 PM   *Ar* CHICAGO 11:00 AM

The Wolverine
(via Michigan Central)
Lv NEW YORK 5:00 PM   *Ar* CHICAGO 12:00 Noon

look in at the Great Steel Fleet, since on that date other Chicago–New York trains were placed on a 20-hour schedule to join the *20th Century Limited*. One was the *Advance 20th Century Limited*; westbound the train ran one hour ahead of the *Century* and eastbound, 40 minutes. This "advance" train was in equipment and services the equal of the main *Century*. Hardly less illustrious was the *Commodore Vanderbilt*, another 20-hour train, which ran about one hour and a quarter behind the *Century*. (These trains were added in part to reduce multiple-section operations of the *Century* itself. In later years there would be an *Advance Commodore Vanderbilt*—all-Pullman, after the *Commodore* itself had begun to carry coaches.) The *Wolverine*, which ran via the Michigan Central, also made the New York–Chicago run in 20 hours. (Like nearly all the trains using the Michigan Central route, the *Wolverine* called at Central Station in Chicago, not La Salle Street.) Eastbound only there was a fifth 20-hour train, the *Fast Mail*, which left Chicago at 9:50 in the morning.

All these trains commanded an extra fare, and others did too. Surcharges of varying amounts also applied to the *Chicago Express*, *Mohawk*, *Cayuga*, *Lake Shore Limited*, *Cleveland Limited*, *Interstate Express*, *Fifth Avenue Special*, *Prairie State*, and *De Witt Clinton* on the old Lake Shore & Michigan Southern route, and the *North Shore Limited*, *Niagara*, and *Eastern Express* on the Michigan Central. Some among this remarkable bevy of trains ran in only one direction, while the extra-fare *Cayuga* and *Iroquois*—both of which ran just westbound—split at Buffalo to send

129

The only water level route between New York and the West

The Literary Digest for August 7, 1926 39

20th Century LIMITED
Chicago–New York New England

Southwestern LIMITED
St. Louis–New York New England

In the historic Hudson River Valley, from a painting by Robert G. Reid.

NEW YORK CENTRAL LINES
Boston & Albany–Michigan Central–Big Four–Pittsburg & Lake Erie
New York Central and Subsidiary Lines

A new illustrated Hudson River booklet, with detailed maps, mailed free to any New York Central Lines Agent or by addressing Department, 466 Lexington Avenue, New York.

sections over both routes. All the 20-hour trains were Pullman-only, as were the *North Shore Limited, Lake Shore Limited, Cleveland Limited, Iroquois, Mohawk,* and *Interstate Limited.* Timings were as long as 25 hours on the southern route, 26 hours and 40 minutes on the northern, but some came in under 22 hours.

So, "all-Pullman, extra-fare" surely didn't apply exclusively to the *20th Century Limited.* The brochure touting these schedule-reductions on the New York–Chicago route called the service "the greatest fleet of fast long-distance passenger trains in the world" and summarized: "nine 20-hour trains, seven in 21 hours or less, sixteen other through Pullman trains." But the flagship would assuredly have the finest, newest cars available—and those special services that set the train aside from all others.

That these notable speed and service upgrades came on September 29, 1929, is surely significant, perhaps ironic. Less than a month later, on October 24, 1929, "Black Thursday," the soaring stock market would crash, the Depression would begin, and things would never be the same

ABOVE: This brochure was issued in June 1949 to promote the newly streamlined *Southwestern Limited*. Compare the dining-car illustration with the one on page 12 showing the 1948 *Century's* diner and notice that the artist simply has removed the horizontal bar motif, so typical of the *Century*, from the partitions in the earlier rendering. In point of fact, the twin-unit diners delivered by Budd for the *Southwestern Limited* were very similar in layout to the *Century's* Pullman-Standard-built twins. ROBERT P. SCHMIDT COLLECTION

RIGHT: In July 1958, back at Terre Haute some three decades after the photograph of the heavyweight *Southwestern Limited* on the facing page was taken, an Electro-Motive E8/E7 combination leads the *Southwestern* eastward. The train has already lost much of its elite status and has even further to fall before the end. WILLARD THOMAS, ROBERT P. SCHMIDT COLLECTION

for American industry, least of all the railroads. Before long, even the proud New York Central would be looking for ways to consolidate services and cut losses.

The *Century* was—and would remain, for a few more decades at least—immune to cuts and changes that would dim its luster. Some other members of the "Fleet" were as well, at least for a time, and prominent among them was the *Southwestern Limited*, the train that for much of its career nearly equaled the *Century* in equipment, priority, and exclusivity. Operating on the Big Four west of Cleveland to St. Louis via Indianapolis, this train, Nos. 11 and 12, actually predated the *Century* and the century, having begun operation in the 1890s. In the heavyweight era, the *Southwestern* drew cars from the same pool as the *Century*. Basically a New York–St. Louis train, it typically had a Cincinnati section, which separated from the St. Louis section in Cleveland, and a Boston

section via the Boston & Albany east of Albany. The train commanded an extra fare, of course, and for a time the Pacifics that hauled it on the CCC&StL part of its run sported plaques on their tenders with the train's name. The *Knickerbocker* to St. Louis and *Ohio State Limited* to Cincinnati were other important New York City trains to operate on the Big Four. (The *Ohio State Limited* would prove the survivor, lasting and operating in some style for as long as there was a Great Steel Fleet.)

When it came time for the *Southwestern Limited* to enter the streamliner era—which it did in 1939, if only partially—its preeminence remained. It shared in a small way (in particular, some *Cascade*-series 10-roomette 5-double bedroom cars) the order that streamlined the *Century* in 1938. More significantly, the only round-end observation cars ordered in this first, prewar round of streamlining for trains other than the *Century* were *Genesee River, Maumee River*, and *Wabash River*—1-compartment 1-drawing room 2-double bedroom buffet-lounge observations delivered in mid 1939 for the *Southwestern Limited*. (These were the cars that in 1942 were transferred to the *Century* to replace *Bedloes Island, Manhattan Island, Pelee Island*, and *Thousand Islands*—cars laid up for the duration of World War II because their single double bedroom and single master room didn't square with the Office of Defense Transportation's minimums for revenue space.)

When it became time for 11 and 12's postwar re-equipping, part of the "30 new Dreamliners" touted in Central publicity throughout the late 1940s, once again the *Southwestern Limited* got premier treatment. It would feature an all-stainless-steel consist, built jointly by the Budd Company and Pullman-Standard. In spite of proposals from Budd at the time, Pullman-Standard had gotten the nod for the 1938 *Century* and the similar sleepers delivered in 1939 and 1940 to partially streamline other members of the Fleet. (These comprised 4-compartment 2-drawing room 4-double bedroom *Imperial*-series cars, 10-roomette 5-double bedroom *Cascade*-series cars, 18-roomette *City*-series cars, and 13-double bedroom *County*-series cars.) After the war, however, possibly to mitigate delivery delays resulting from the backlog of orders and the need for the railway-car industry to retool, NYC split its orders among various builders, and Budd got a good deal of the action, including some entire trains.

The *Southwestern Limited* re-equipping was completed in mid 1949. Pulled by Electro-Motive E7-model diesel-electric locomotives, this train gained its greatest distinction at the other end, with its 5-double bedroom buffet-lounge observation cars, of which there were three: *Singing Brook*,

The spring of 1948 was an interesting moment in the evolution of motive power for the Great Steel Fleet. Electro-Motive E7s had arrived and already were running routinely on the *Century* (then just five months away from receiving new and refurbished rolling stock) and other trains. Dreyfuss-styled streamlined Hudsons remained much in evidence, supplemented by the more powerful Niagaras (tucked away behind the diesels on the cover of this brochure). The timetable and map inside show that the postwar Fleet remains formidable. PETER V. TILP COLLECTION

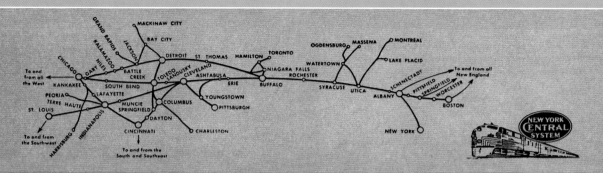

NEW YORK • TOLEDO • CHICAGO

Standard Time	The Mohawk 5	North Shore Limited 39	The Pacemaker 1	Advance Commodore Vanderbilt 65	Commodore Vanderbilt 67	20th Century Limited 25	The Water Level 63	The Wolverine 17	Lake Shore Limited 19	The Chicagoan 59
New York (Grand Cent. Term.)....(ET) Lv.	9:00 am	12:00 N'n	3:00 pm	3:15 pm	3:45 pm	5:00 pm	5:05 pm	6:05 pm	6:30 pm	11:00 pm
Harmon........Lv.	9:48 am	12:50 pm	3:46 pm	4:01 pm	4:31 pm	5:46 pm	5:51 pm	6:51 pm	7:18 pm	11:48 pm
Toledo........Ar.	3:05 am	Via Detroit	3:57 am	4:05 am	4:24 am	....	6:16 am	Via Detroit	8:30 am	11:48 am
South Bend........(CT) Ar.	5:00 am		f5:20 am	5:33 am	5:45 am	....	7:50 am		10:15 am	1:15 pm
Englewood........Ar.	6:42 am		6:51 am	7:00 am	7:25 am	7:45 am	9:05 am		11:59 am	2:45 pm
Chicago (LaSalle St. Station)........Ar.	6:55 am		7:05 am	7:15 am	7:40 am	8:00 am	9:20 am		12:15 pm	3:00 pm
Woodlawn (63rd St.)........Ar.	....	8:15 am	Reserved Seat Coaches	....	Sleeping Cars Only	Sleeping Cars Only	....	11:05 am	....	....
Chicago (Central Station)........Ar.	....	8:30 am		....			....	11:15 am	....	....

f Stops on signal to receive or discharge certain long distance passengers. See your local ticket agent for full details.

CHICAGO • TOLEDO • NEW YORK

Standard Time	New York Special 44	Fifth Avenue Special 6	Advance Commodore Vanderbilt 66	The Wolverine 8	Commodore Vanderbilt 68	The Pacemaker 2	20th Century Limited 26	The Water Level 64	The Mohawk 10	Lake Shore Limited 22	North Shore Limited 40	The Chicagoan 90
Chicago (LaSalle St. Station)......(CT) Lv.	....	11:20 am	1:30 pm	....	3:00 pm	3:30 pm	4:00 pm	4:40 pm	5:15 pm	6:15 pm	....	11:00 pm
Englewood........Lv.	....	11:35 am	1:44 pm	....	3:14 pm	3:44 pm	4:14 pm	4:54 pm	5:29 pm	6:29 pm	....	11:14 pm
Chicago (Central Station)........Lv.	8:45 am	....	Sleeping Cars Only	2:15 pm	Sleeping Cars Only	Reserved Seat Coaches	Sleeping Cars Only	....	....	....	10:20 pm	....
Woodlawn (63rd St)........Lv.	8:57 am	....		2:25 pm				....	....	....	10:30 pm	....
South Bend........Lv.	Via Detroit	12:45 pm	2:54 pm	Via Detroit		f4:51 pm		6:10 pm	6:55 pm	7:35 pm	via Detroit	f12:26 am
Toledo........(ET) Lv.		4:20 pm	6:15 pm		f7:38 pm	f8:10 pm	....	9:50 pm	11:50 pm	11:05 pm		4:00 am
Harmon........Ar.	5:42 am	5:52 am	6:07am	8:22 am	7:26 am	8:11 am	7:32 am	11:52 pm	2:17 pm	11:17 pm	6:18 pm	5:07 pm
New York (Grand Central Terminal)....Ar.	6:40 am	6:50 am	7:05 am	9:20 am	8:25 am	9:05 am	8:30 am	12:50 pm	3:15 pm	12:15 pm	7:15 pm	6:00 pm

f Stops on signal to receive or discharge certain long distance passengers. See your local ticket agent for full details.

Sunrise Brook, and *Wingate Brook*. These cars were essentially Budd's version of Pullman-Standard's *Creek*-series cars, including step-up Lookout Lounges. Inside they were virtually indistinguishable, and their parity is suggested by the fact that, in the 1960s when *Sandy Creek* or *Hickory Creek* was rotated out of the consist for shopping, *Sunrise Brook* and more often *Wingate Brook* stood in admirably (page 121). The *Southwestern Limited* also echoed the *Century* of the period in carrying a twin-unit diner.

But for all the radiance of its heavyweight years and first years as a streamliner, the train finally lost its luster before some other members of the Great Steel Fleet. As the 1950s wore on, Nos. 11 and 12 evolved into a six-days-a week St. Louis–Cleveland train with through sleepers and coaches for New York (carried by the *Cleveland Limited*) and Boston (carried by the *New England States*)—sans observation car, sans lounge car. The train even lost the "Limited" from its name, becoming just the *Southwestern*.

Two of the postwar "Dreamliners" that were pure Budd trains were the all-coach New York–Chicago *Pacemaker* and the Boston–Chicago *New England States*. The *Pacemaker* has an especially interesting history. It was hastily launched on July 28, 1939, to match up with the Pennsylvania Railroad's coaches-only luxury *Trailblazer*. (Even the "Pacemaker" name seems somewhat emulative.) Carrying the marker lamps initially were a pair of open-platform observation cars—*Seneca Valley* and *Catskill*

Valley—released from *Century* service by the 1938 streamlining, converted at the Big Four's Beech Grove Shops and painted in two tones of gray.

The train, originally carrying numbers 2 and 3, later switched to 1 and 2, ran on a 17-hour schedule, just an hour slower than the *Century*, with departure times similar to 25 and 26's in both directions. "Luxury travel at bargain fares" was the claim of this "spic-and-span gray flyer" that "sets the pace for luxurious coach travel between New York and

Motive-power multiplicity is again illustrated in this Leslie Ragan painting titled "For the Public Service." The La Salle Street Station scene appeared on New York Central's 1946 calendar. BILL STRASSNER COLLECTION

134

Chicago." Amenities listed, in addition to speed, included complete air-conditioning, an observation-buffet-lounge car (with radio), a mid-train club-buffet-lounge car, all-reserved reclining seats at no extra charge, dining car "serving New York Central meals famous for their excellence: Breakfast 50¢, luncheon 65¢, dinner 75¢," a coach "for the exclusive use of women and children," magazines, and "uniformed attendants to render personal service."

The open-platform observation cars ran until September 1940, when they were replaced by enclosed observation-lounges Nos. 53 and 56, rebuilt since they had run on the New York–Buffalo *Day Coach Deluxe*. These cars were unique, curious hybrids—monitor-roofed heavyweights with the rounded observation ends ushered in by the streamline era. In *Pacemaker* service, they and the balance of the heavyweight trains wore a yellow-striped brown livery. The fare actually dropped slightly, to $27.25 round trip between New York and Chicago.

The next edition of the *Pacemaker* was the postwar Budd train, assembled from equipment delivered from late 1946 through early 1948. Coaches were among a fleet of sixty 56-seat chair cars. Mid-train there was a twin-unit diner-lounge, and at the rear a tavern-lounge observation. A brochure from December 1947 promises "two smart club cars. The forward diner-lounge has deep, inviting easy chairs and big panorama windows. The luxurious rear-end Observation Car offers these plus radio . . . writing desk . . . card tables . . . a refreshment bar . . . and all-the-way-round rear-view windows, with divans for lazing and gazing." This truly was a worthy economy-minded running mate to the extra-fare, all-Pullman *Century*, itself about to be largely re-equipped.

The Boston–Chicago *New England States*, train Nos. 27 and 28, which about this same time

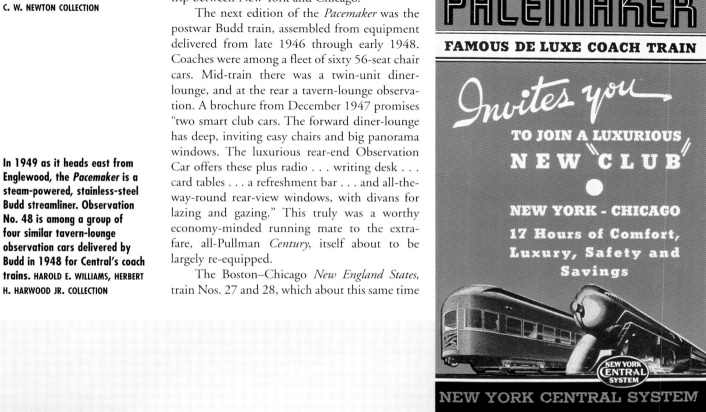

RIGHT: This *Pacemaker* brochure dates from the era of Central's idiosyncratic, homebuilt heavyweight solarium cars, introduced in the fall of 1940. C. W. NEWTON COLLECTION

In 1949 as it heads east from Englewood, the *Pacemaker* is a steam-powered, stainless-steel Budd streamliner. Observation No. 48 is among a group of four similar tavern-lounge observation cars delivered by Budd in 1948 for Central's coach trains. HAROLD E. WILLIAMS, HERBERT H. HARWOOD JR. COLLECTION

would be unveiled in new dress courtesy of Budd, had come into being with the 1938 streamlining of the *Century*, replacing the Boston section of that train. Essentially a heavyweight train in its first decade, 27 and 28 did receive some of the streamlined sleepers that arrived from Pullman-Standard in 1939 and 1940. This allowed the train, which also carried coaches, to offer the full panoply of sleeping accommodations: compartments, bedrooms, drawing rooms, roomettes, and sections—something for everyone.

When the fully streamlined version of the train appeared in 1949, its feature cars were 5-double bedroom buffet-lounge observations *Babbling Brook* and *Bonnie Brook*. (Identical *Fall Brook* and *Plum Brook* went to the *Ohio State Limited*. All four of these cars were akin to the *Southwestern Limited*'s *Brook* cars, but without the deep-windowed Lookout Lounge.) This stainless-steel train carried *Valley*-series 10-roomette 6-double bedroom sleepers and, initially, a *Stream*-series 6-double bedroom buffet-lounge mid-train and two grill diners. In 1952 twin-unit diners were assigned; the kitchen car contained a lounge section, so the bedroom-lounges were then dropped from the consist. The train carried coaches too. The 1949 brochure that covered the re-equipping was titled "The *New England States*—first all-room dreamliner between New England and the Midwest," but a band in the upper-right-hand corner read "More good news! Luxury coaches too, on the all-new *New England States*."

Back in 1929, when Central's fleet of 20-hour trains was expanded to nine, the *Wolverine* was one of them, and it remained

RIGHT: This June 1949 brochure for the streamlining of the *New England States* highlighted the train's features, including its regional cuisine. ROBERT P. SCHMIDT COLLECTION

Alco PA-type locomotives speed the Budd-built *New England States* through Palmer, Mass., in 1951. (The camera's curtain shutter has given the locomotive's nose a rakish slant.) The lanky, handsome PAs are leaving behind a substantial trail of exhaust, the characteristic that led them to be dubbed "honorary steam locomotives" by railfans. S. K. BOLTON JR., HERBERT H. HARWOOD JR. COLLECTION

MORE GOOD NEWS!
Luxury coaches too, on the all-new "NEW ENGLAND STATES"

"The New England States"

first all-room dreamliner between New England and the Midwest

BOSTON & ALBANY ROUTE
of the
NEW YORK CENTRAL SYSTEM

Take Your Pick of the Pack!

World's greatest fleet of newly-equipped trains is ready _now_ to speed you home for the holidays!

CLEVELAND LIMITED
CLEVELAND · NEW YORK

SOUTHWESTERN LIMITED
NEW YORK · BOSTON
INDIANAPOLIS · ST. LOUIS

EMPIRE STATE EXPRESS
NEW YORK · BUFFALO
CLEVELAND · DETROIT

OHIO STATE LIMITED
CINCINNATI · DAYTON
COLUMBUS · NEW YORK

THE PACEMAKER
CHICAGO · TOLEDO
CLEVELAND · NEW YORK

THE MERCURY
CHICAGO
DETROIT · CLEVELAND

NEW ENGLAND STATES
CHICAGO · BOSTON

COMMODORE VANDERBILT
CHICAGO · NEW YORK

THE DETROITER
NEW YORK · DETROIT

JAMES WHITCOMB RILEY
CHICAGO
INDIANAPOLIS · CINCINNATI

TWILIGHT LIMITED
CHICAGO · DETROIT

20TH CENTURY LIMITED
CHICAGO · NEW YORK

Leaders of New York Central's Great Passenger Fleet

Enjoy the New in New York Central! Glide homeward in new luxury coaches or private-room sleeping cars, behind smooth Diesel-electric locomotives. Feast in new diners. Join in the holiday fun aboard new lounge cars. From end to end of New York Central, you'll find world's largest orders for new, streamlined equipment are filled at last!

Leave Weather out of your Plans! Let storms sweep the skyways. Let sleet snarl holiday traffic on the highways. Aboard your New York Central daylight streamliner or overnight Dreamliner, you can settle back with a free mind and enjoy every minute. For you're traveling the world's safest way. And you *know* you'll get there as planned ... *weather or no!*

This year, make a Holiday Homecoming your Gift! There's no present like the presence of loved ones around the family Christmas tree. So send tickets for a trip home as *your* gift. Ask your New York Central ticket agent how to send tickets and reservations. Ask, too, about money-saving round-trip fares.

NEW NEW YORK CENTRAL
The Water Level Route—You Can Sleep

NEW YORK CENTRAL SYSTEM

the premier train on the Michigan Central route via Detroit and Canada right to the end, with coaches and Pullmans serving both New York and Boston for most of its career. By the eve of World War II, though it remained basically a heavyweight train, it carried a few lightweight sleepers, which allowed it to offer roomettes—much in the ascendancy by then, dramatically outdistancing berths (uppers particularly) in acceptance by the traveling public. Complete streamlining came when the railroad's huge postwar orders for passenger cars were filled.

continued on page 141

137

NEW through Coast to Coast Sleeping C

between NEW YORK · LOS ANGELES · SAN

NEW YORK — LOS ANGELES
DAILY VIA
NEW YORK CENTRAL — SANTA FE ROUTE

20th Century Limited—The Chief
(Eastbound and Westbound)

Westbound Example READ DOWN		DAILY, EXTRA-FARE SERVICE			Eastbound Example READ UP
Fri.	5:00 PM	Lv. New York (Grand Cent. Term.) NYC (ET)	Ar.		8:30 AM Mon.
"	5:46 PM	" Harmon	"	Ar.	7:34 AM Mon.
"	7:37 PM	" Albany	"	Ar.	5:27 AM Mon.
"	10:02 PM	" Syracuse	"		
Sat.	8:00 AM	Ar. Chicago (LaSalle St. Sta.)	(CT)	Lv.	3:30 PM Sun.
"	12:01 PM	Lv. Chicago (Dearborn Sta.)	AT&SF	Ar.	1:00 PM Sun.
"	9:40 PM	Ar. Kansas City, Mo.			3:55 AM Sun.
Sun.	6:40 AM	" La Junta, Colo.			4:50 PM Sat.
"	2:45 PM	" Albuquerque, N. Mex.			9:00 AM Sat.
"	10:10 PM	" Williams, Ariz.			1:10 AM "
"	11:55 PM	" Ash Fork, Ariz.			12:01 AM Sat.
Mon.	5:40 AM	" Barstow, Calif.		(PT)	3:50 PM Fri.
"	8:05 AM	" San Bernardino, Calif.			1:45 PM "
"	9:30 AM	" Pasadena, Calif.			12:30 PM "
Mon.	10:00 AM	" Los Angeles, Calif.		Lv.	12:01 PM Fri.

NEW YORK-LOS ANGELES (4 Compartment-4Double Bedroom-2 Drawing Room) Car 2501.
LOS ANGELES-NEW YORK (4 Compartment-4Double Bedroom-2 Drawing Room) Car 2601.

From coast to coast your through all-room car is always surrounded by the luxurious dining, lounge and observation facilities of these nationally famous premium-fare trains . . . The 20th Century Limited and The Chief.

Seen by daylight are the romantic panorama of the Hudson River Valley, the fertile prairies of Indiana and Illinois, the majesty of mighty Raton pass, the Indian pageantry at New Mexican stops, colorful Cajon Pass and California's lovely orange groves.

Your terminals provide utmost convenience and ease of travel —in New York you arrive or leave in beautiful Grand Central Terminal in the heart of the city, and in Los Angeles the new Union Station, so centrally located to all Los Angeles county.

NEW YORK — LOS ANGELES
DAILY VIA
NEW YORK CENTRAL — OVERLAND ROUTE

Commodore Vanderbilt—Transcontinental Limited
(Eastbound and Westbound)

Westbound Example READ DOWN		DAILY			Eastbound Example READ UP
Fri.	3:45 PM	Lv. New York (Grand Cent. Term.) NYC (ET)	Ar.		8:30 AM Mon.
"	4:31 PM	" Harmon	"	Ar.	7:27 AM Mon.
Sat.	7:45 AM	Ar. Chicago (LaSalle St. Sta.)	NYC (CT)	Lv.	2:30 PM Sun.
"	11:00 AM	Lv. Chicago (C&NW Sta.)	C&NW	Ar.	12:15 PM "
"	8:40 PM	Ar. Omaha, Nebr.	"	Lv.	2:35 AM Sun.
Sun.	5:35 AM	" Cheyenne, Wyo.	UP	(MT)	4:25 PM Sat.
"	7:15 AM	" Laramie, Wyo.	"	"	2:40 PM "
"	9:33 AM	" Rawlins, Wyo.	"	"	12:20 PM "
"	4:15 PM	" Ogden, Utah	"	"	5:50 AM "
"	5:20 PM	" Salt Lake City, Utah	"	"	4:45 AM Sat.
Mon.	2:00 AM	" Las Vegas, Nev.	"	(PT)	4:00 PM Fri.
"	4:25 AM	" San Bernardino, Calif.	"	"	11:50 AM "
"	8:45 AM	" Riverside, Calif.	"	"	11:27 AM "
Mon.	10:20 AM	" Los Angeles, Calif.	"	"	10:00 AM Fri.

NEW YORK-LOS ANGELES (8 Section-6 Double Bedroom) Car 6704.
LOS ANGELES-NEW YORK (8 Section-6 Double Bedroom) Car 45.

Convenient mid-morning arrival at destination is provided by the popular Commodore Vanderbilt and the new Transcontinental Limited.

Daylight hours westbound offer the beauty of the Hudson River Valley, the well-kept green farmlands of Illinois and Iowa, the Rockies of Wyoming, Utah's crested Wasatch Range, Great Salt Lake and the spreading fruit orchards of California.

Eastbound, the traveler sees the quickly changing scenery of flowering orchards, snow-capped peaks and wierd desert plants of the Mojave, the mountains and cattle ranges of Wyoming, the shores of the Great Lakes . . . all climaxed by an inspiring early morning ride for miles along the banks of the Hudson River.

NEW YORK — LOS ANGELES
EVERY OTHER DAY VIA
NEW YORK CENTRAL — GOLDEN STATE ROUTE

Iroquois — Golden State Limited (Westbound)
Golden State Limited—Commodore Vanderbilt (Eastbound)

Westbound Example READ DOWN		EVERY OTHER DAY			Eastbound Example READ UP
Fri.	11:15 PM	Lv. New York (Grand Cent. Term.) NYC (ET)	Ar.		8:30 AM Mon.
Sat.	12:03 AM	" Harmon	"	Ar.	7:27 AM Mon.
"	7:15 AM	" Buffalo	"	"	
"	10:03 PM	" Syracuse	"	"	
"	11:24 PM	" Utica	"	"	5:14 AM "
Sat.	12:23 AM	" Syracuse	"	"	4:20 AM "
"	3:14 AM	" Buffalo	"	"	1:50 AM Mon.
"	6:55 AM	" Cleveland			
Sun.	8:25 AM	Ar. Kansas City, Mo.		Lv.	3:10 AM Sun.
"	8:20 PM	" Tucumcari, N. Mex.			3:50 PM Sat.
Mon.	2:10 AM	" El Paso, Tex.	SP	(MT)	8:10 AM "
"	9:16 AM	" Tucson, Ariz.	"	"	12:35 AM Sat.
"	11:55 AM	" Phoenix, Ariz.	"	"	10:00 PM Fri.
"	5:58 PM	" Palm Springs, Calif.	"	(PT)	1:55 PM "
Mon.	8:45 PM	" Los Angeles, Calif.	"	"	11:15 AM Fri.

NEW YORK-LOS ANGELES (4 Compartment-4 Double Bedroom-2 Drawing Room) Car 5902.
LOS ANGELES-NEW YORK (4 Compartment-4 Double Bedroom-2 Drawing Room) Car 42.

Featured by the westbound combination of the Iroquois-Golden State Limited is the convenient after-theatre departure from Grand Central Terminal with early evening arrival in Los Angeles. Eastbound, the Golden State Limited and the famous Commodore Vanderbilt, give early morning arrival in the heart of New York.

Daytime travel in both directions extends through the Great Lakes region, the grain-rich prairies of Kansas and western Oklahoma, the irrigation projects, mountains and mining country of New Mexico and Arizona and the valley resorts near Los Angeles.

Approaching New York, as fitting end to any cross-continent trip, the early riser may view the glories of the majestic Hudson River Valley.

NEW YORK — SAN FRANCISCO
DAILY VIA
NEW YORK CENTRAL — OVERLAND ROUTE

Lake Shore Limited—Overland Limited (Westbound)
Overland Limited—Water Level Limited (Eastbound)

Westbound Example READ DOWN		DAILY			Eastbound Example READ UP
Fri.	6:30 PM	Lv. New York (Grand Cent. Term.) NYC (ET)	Ar.		10:00 AM Mon.
"	7:18 PM	" Harmon	"	Ar.	9:05 AM "
"	9:53 PM	" Schenectady	"	"	6:56 AM "
"	10:05 PM	" Schenectady	"	"	6:50 AM "
"	11:24 PM	" Utica	"	"	5:14 AM "
Sat.	12:23 AM	" Syracuse	"	"	4:20 AM "
"	3:14 AM	" Buffalo	"	"	1:50 AM Mon.
"	6:55 AM	" Cleveland	"	"	
"	1:00 PM	Ar. Chicago (LaSalle St. Sta.)	(CT)	Lv.	4:00 PM "
"	3:00 PM	Lv. Chicago (C&NW Sta.)	C&NW	Ar.	2:00 PM "
Sun.	12:35 AM	Ar. Omaha, Nebr.	UP	Lv.	4:20 AM Sun.
"	9:38 AM	" Cheyenne, Wyo.	"	"	7:16 AM Sat.
"	6:20 PM	" Ogden, Utah	"	"	7:18 AM Sat.
Mon.	6:30 AM	" Reno, Nev.	SP	(PT)	7:38 PM Fri.
"	11:30 AM	" Sacramento, Calif.	"	"	2:20 PM "
"	1:42 PM	" Oakland, Calif. (16th St.)	"	"	1:10 PM "
Mon.	2:20 PM	" San Francisco, Calif.	"	"	11:30 AM Fri.

NEW YORK-SAN FRANCISCO (8 Section-1 Drawing Room-2 Compartment) Car 1927.
SAN FRANCISCO-NEW YORK (8 Section-1 Drawing Room-2 Compartment) Car 268.

Dinnertime departure westbound with an after lunch arrival in San Francisco are advantages offered travelers via the Lake Shore Limited-Overland Limited through sleeping car. Eastbound mid-day departure from San Francisco via the Overland Limited and Water Level Limited allows mid-morning arrival at Grand Central Terminal.

Highlights for San Francisco bound passengers are the Hudson River by twilight, the Great Lakes country, the summits of the Rockies in Wyoming and the early morning view of Donner Summit, Donner Lake and Cape Horn in the Sierra high country before entering the American and Sacramento River valleys. Added attractions eastbound are the Lucin cutoff over Great Salt Lake at dawn and the morning ride through the historic Hudson River Valley.

BELOW: Transcontinental through cars provided intriguing variety for those who paid attention to the look of passenger trains as they rolled by, since off-line cars often stood out in otherwise matched consists. The glint of stainless steel in an all-gray *Commodore Vanderbilt*, for instance, wouldn't go unnoticed. In this view of the eastbound *Commodore* departing Englewood in the summer of 1948, a stainless-and-vermilion Rock Island sleeper off the *Golden State* and one of four Budd-built twin-unit diner sets acquired from Chesapeake & Ohio are in sharp contrast to somber, stately NYC livery. ANDREW M. SPIEKER

ABOVE AND FACING PAGE (COVER INSET): This June 2, 1946, folder shows the impressive scope of NYC's through-Pullman operations in the inaugural summer of these services. Sleepers operating through the "great wall of Chicago" never caught on as well as expected, perhaps because of the laborious switching moves required to transfer through cars not only between different terminals in some cases, but out of one train consist and into another. Such switching moves were not only expensive for the carriers but boring for patrons who had chosen to remain aboard the cars. WILLIAM F. HOWES JR. COLLECTION

A choice of through

COAST TO COAST

SLEEPING CAR SERVICES

on
favorite trains
of
famous routes

NEW YORK CENTRAL SYSTEM

NEW YORK CENTRAL

Effective June 2, 1946

Coast-to-coast sleeping-car service, finally inaugurated on March 31, 1946, was long in gestation, and for a time there had even been serious discussion of through transcontinental trains. As far back as 1937, New York Central and Pennsy had contemplated New York—Los Angeles service via Chicago in partnership with Santa Fe or the Overland Route railroads (Union Pacific and Chicago & North Western). Though it never happened, this was not as radical an idea as it might seem. Certainly the NYC had experience operating through trains in collaboration with other railroads; the Pennsy had perhaps even more, being the Washington—New York link for the Atlantic Coast Line, Seaboard Air Line, Southern Railway, and Chesapeake & Ohio and participating in other interline arrangements.

But a transcontinental train proved an elusive concept, with World War II intervening before such talk could become anything more than just that. After the war, however, planning picked up again, though ultimately toward a more modest goal: transcontinental sleeping cars transferred at Chicago. When such service began, the *20th Century Limited* was a participant, carrying a through car for Los Angeles to be conveyed in Santa Fe's *Chief*. So was PRR's *Broadway Limited*, which also carried a car for the *Chief*. At this point in the great Pennsy-Central rivalry, parity was a given.

A catalyst of sorts, and a central part of the lore of transcontinental Pullmans, was Robert R. Young, who became chairman of the New York Central in 1954 after a bitter proxy fight. The previous decade, while chairman of the Chesapeake & Ohio, he promoted advertisements condemning the need for coast-to-coast passengers to change trains in Chicago. "A hog can cross the country without changing trains," bannered the ad, "but YOU can't!" No doubt this public taunting provided some additional incentive for executives at the big players like Pennsy and Central and Santa Fe to get transcontinental Pullmans into their trains.

By the summer of 1946, the Central was participating in no fewer than five New York City—California routes. The *Century* sent a sleeper to Los Angeles via the *Chief*, and the *Commodore Vanderbilt* teamed with the *Transcontinental Limited* on the Overland Route to Los Angeles. The Golden State Route—Chicago, Rock Island & Pacific and Southern Pacific—also hosted a Los Angeles car, on the *Golden State*, carried by Central's *Iroquois* westbound and *Commodore Vanderbilt* eastbound.

To San Francisco, a Pullman was carried by the *San Francisco Overland* across the C&NW, UP, and Southern Pacific; it moved over the Central in the *Lake Shore Limited* westbound and the *Water Level Limited* eastbound. The *Exposition Flyer*, which ran on the Chicago, Burlington & Quincy, Denver & Rio Grande Western, and Western Pacific, also carried a San Francisco (Oakland, actually) car. Within the year this through service would be inherited by the *Exposition Flyer's* successor, the *California Zephyr*, and the heavyweight 10-section 1-drawing room 2-compartment Pullman replaced by a lightweight 10-roomette 6-double bedroom car. On the Central, the through car was initially carried on the *Commodore Vanderbilt*. (Train assignments for through cars varied considerably through the years.)

Baltimore & Ohio's through cars from Washington for the *Chief* added to this rich stew; the resulting car shuffle in Chicago was impressive, involving Union Station, Dearborn Station, Grand Central, North Western Terminal, as well as La Salle Street. In some cases cars had to be pulled, moved between stations, cleaned, serviced, and re-spotted in under two hours, a daunting task. Passengers were welcome to stay aboard during this process if they chose, but many opted to stretch their legs and take a quick took at Chicago.

The through Pullmans never were an overwhelming success. Staying aboard the cars during switching was a mixed blessing. Not having to handle luggage was a welcome convenience, but Parmalee Transfer routinely offered a service to move luggage among stations, sleeper to sleeper, so even that advantage was muted. Still, it was the general constriction of passenger-train services and amenities that ushered out the coast-to-coast cars. On the NYC, by the time the *Century-Chief* car (by then carried on the *Super Chief*) was dropped in the early spring of 1958, all the other lines had vanished, many of them years before.

NEW YORK CENTRAL SYSTEM

continued from page 137

As the 1950s began, the Fleet still sailed with some authority between the Midwest and New York and Boston. Along with the *Wolverine*, the *North Shore Limited* westbound and the *New York Special* eastbound continued to serve the Michigan Central/Canada Southern routing. On the New York Central main line via Toledo and Cleveland, the *20th Century Limited* and *Commodore Vanderbilt* (both of them all-Pullman) were joined by the *Advance Commodore Vanderbilt* and *Pacemaker* (by then operated as one train but listed separately in the timetable), *New England States*, *Lake Shore Limited*, *Chicagoan* (serving New York westbound and both New York and Boston eastbound), *Fifth Avenue Special* eastbound to New York, the *Iroquois* westbound from Boston, and *Interstate Express* eastbound to Boston.

As the 1950s concluded, much of the Fleet remained afloat, but the seas had roughened dramatically and the sky was decidedly red at morning, as losses on passenger trains mounted inexorably. By the 1960s, NYC President Alfred Perlman's policy of diminution and downgrading of passenger service to stop the financial bleeding was progressing full speed ahead, the one happy exception being the *20th Century Limited*'s enhancements in time for it's 60th birthday in 1962.

What was left of the Great Steel Fleet finally sank definitively on Dec. 2, 1967, with the *Century* by far the most celebrated casualty. (Effective Nov. 5, 1967, it had been combined with the *New England States* west of Buffalo.) Foundering in the same seas, however, were other familiar names, although in some cases their operating routines had been shuffled: the *Wolverine*, still a New York–Detroit–Chicago train; the *Empire State Express*, now having been extended all the way to Chicago, westbound via Cleveland and eastbound via Detroit; the *Chicagoan* and, eastbound only, the *Fifth Avenue-Cleveland Limited* serving Chicago–Cleveland–New York; the *Iroquois*, truncated to a New York–Buffalo run; the *Cayuga*, still a New York–Buffalo train; and the *Twilight Limited*, now only a Chicago–Detroit run. The *Ohio State Limited* had already lost its name, as had the *Southwestern*—its sad remnant now but a St. Louis–Union City, Ind., local, and the *Knickerbocker* having evolved into NYC's premier St. Louis train. Effective with the Dec. 2 bloodbath, the new order east of Buffalo would be an anonymous, amenity-free fleet of coach trains dubbed "Empire Service." West to Chicago, one nameless train would run on roughly the *20th Century Limited* and *New England States*' schedule, but the red carpet, *Creek* cars, and virtually every other special thing that had made New York Central passenger trains great was packed away—forever.

BELOW: Three Electro-Motive locomotives—two E7As and a "Geep"—power the eastbound *Wolverine* as it arrives at Englewood on July 29, 1967, with a full complement of coaches, sleepers, and a diner-lounge. In earlier years, the presence of a diesel road-switcher in a motive-power consist for so illustrious a member of the Fleet as the *Wolverine* would have been unthinkable. MIKE SCHAFER

Keeping a watchful eye on his train and its passengers, the conductor of the *Ohio State Limited* performs a visual inspection as the Cincinnati-bound streamliner sweeps through Fonda, N.Y., in the Mohawk River valley. A heavyweight lounge car ahead of the diner subs for regularly assigned lightweight equipment. JIM SHAUGHNESSY

141

OTHER FLEETS: THE COMPETITION

hough some would say that the *20th Century Limited* had no peers, Philadelphians and particularly residents of the exclusive Main Line suburbs of that city might strenuously make a case for the *Broadway Limited* as the best New York–Chicago service. The two trains went head-to-head right from the beginning, operating on always-equal timings with similar equipment and amenities. They served the same endpoints (and both trains were operated primarily for this long-distance business), though they took much different

Near Englewood, Ill., where the tracks of the Pennsylvania Railroad and the New York Central paralleled each other briefly on their otherwise widely divergent paths between Chicago and New York, this classic race between the *Broadway Limited* and the *Century* was a possibility on any given morning or evening. Powered by one of the Pennsy's famous K4 Pacifics in this circa 1930 scene, the *Broadway* has a slight lead over the Hudson-powered *Century*. This dramatic image of two great lines' most emblematic locomotives at full gallop with flagships in tow speaks volumes about what may have been the industry's most intense rivalry ever. PETER V. TILP COLLECTION

Broad Way Limited
PENNSYLVANIA RAILROAD

SPEED AND SECURITY

routes along the way. The PRR had a significantly shorter route (902 as opposed to 961 miles), but it involved climbing the Allegheny Mountains with the help of Horseshoe Curve, so it ended up balancing evenly with NYC's largely grade-free Water Level Route. PRR benefited from serving Philadelphia at convenient times, and in fact the *Broadway* could be considered as much a Philadelphia train as a New York City train. Albany, capital of New York State and the Central's analogous city, was much less defining of the *Century*'s personality than Philadelphia of the *Broadway Limited*'s.

Certainly the NYC and the PRR were fierce rivals, though the story of their passenger trains often shows them operating in an oddly collaborative manner. However, an episode from the 1880s makes clear just how cutthroat the railroads' relationship was in that early period. New York Central & Hudson River president William H. Vanderbilt (son and heir to Cornelius, the Commodore) was angered that PRR had control of the New York, West Shore & Buffalo, a directly competing line right across the Hudson River from the NYC&HR. He fought back by beginning the South Pennsylvania, a classic "nuisance" line that would directly parallel the PRR across Pennsylvania. This overbuilding was bad for the markets, however, so J. P. Morgan—a hugely powerful banker who sat on the NYC&HR

board—took matters in his own hands. In July 1885 he took Pennsy president George Roberts and Central president Chauncey Depew (who had taken over from Vanderbilt just the month before) out onto the Hudson aboard *Corsair*, his yacht. Legend has it that he refused to return to shore until the two men had agreed to end their bitter, unfruitful competition. As a result, NYC&HR acquired the West Shore and PRR the South Penn—which was never completed and, 65 years later, contributed tunnels and grading to the Pennsylvania Turnpike, the country's first superhighway.

The two railroads continued to measure themselves against each other, of course, so when the 20-hour *20th Century Limited* was inaugurated on June 15, 1902, the PRR had to have an answer, which was the *Pennsylvania Special*, begun the same day, on the same schedule. The *Pennsylvania Limited*, much like the Central's *Lake Shore Limited*, had previously been the flagship and would continue in a lesser role right up to

Amtrak's inception. The name *Broadway Limited* came in 1912 and in the early years was rendered *Broad Way Limited*. (It's said that the train was actually named for the Pennsy's six-track New York–Philadelphia main line, rather than the famous Manhattan avenue.)

One intriguing aspect of the competition, passed on only anecdotally, is Central's contemplation of a Philadelphia section of the *Century* to tap that substantial market always securely held by Pennsy. The plan, said to have been floated in the early 1920s, a time when any kind of

Published shortly after the *Broadway*'s 1948 re-equipping (which paralleled the *Century*'s, of course), this brochure highlights the train's feature cars and sleeping accommodations. In this spread, the train's new twin-unit diner is shown. The 1948 *Century* also carried a twin-unit dining car. KARL ZIMMERMANN COLLECTION

SO INVITING —

THE *Master Dining Car*

You'll detect it the moment you enter . . . sense its significance when the steward greets you. New beauty . . . new spaciousness . . . the *Broadway Limited*'s traditional high standard of courteous, meticulous service . . . the festive experience of dining out and the anticipation of delicious food—served you by carefully trained personnel. Pastel-shaded linens, gleaming silverware, the soft harmony of color and charm, the diversified menu—*there's a new treat in dining awaiting you here!*

Fine foods are prepared in the *Broadway Limited's* modern stainless steel kitchen—located in an adjoining car.

expansion seemed possible, had the train setting out from Philadelphia over the Reading Railroad to Newberry Junction, just west of Williamsport, Pa. Reaching Central rails there, the train would travel northwest to the main line, where it would be added to the New York/Boston *Century* or perhaps run independently to Chicago. In any case, the Philadelphia *Century* was never anything but talk, and it's hard to know at this distance how serious the talk was, given the secondary nature of much of the track the train would have traveled. President Alfred Smith's untimely death in 1924, when he fell from his horse in New York's Central Park, apparently ended the project.

Throughout the heavyweight years, the *Broadway* kept pace with the *Century* in timings and services but consistently fell far short in sections operated. The streamline era underlined even more dramatically the collaborative nature of the passenger planning by Central and Pennsy. The 1937 announcement of the streamlined *20th Century Limited* was made jointly by NYC, PRR, and Pullman and also unveiled the Pennsy's "Fleet of Modernism," led by a new *Broadway Limited* but including the Washington–Chicago *Liberty Limited*, the New York–St. Louis "*Spirit of St. Louis*," and *The General* between New York and Chicago, PRR's answer to New York Central's *Commodore Vanderbilt*.

The following year the *Century* and *Broadway* were inaugurated simultaneously. Industrial designer Raymond Loewy's colorful designs for the *Broadway* placed the train in dramatic aesthetic contrast to Dreyfuss' *Century* with its striking metallic hues, but the services offered were essentially identical. The two roads shared the distinction of fielding the country's first all-room trains and later initiating a 15½-hour schedule between New York and Chicago that has yet to be topped (Amtrak's feeble *Broadway* descendant, the *Three Rivers*, and the ex-NYC-routed *Lake Shore Limited* both require around 19 hours).

The trains continued neck-and-neck with the post-World War II re-equippings. Both had twin-unit diners, mid-train lounges with shower, barber shop, and train secretary, and luxurious observations—*Mountain View* and *Tower View* in the case of the *Broadway*. And though the *Broadway*'s long slide down from that point was more linear than the *Century*'s, lacking that train's late-1950s valley and early-1960s peak, it ended at the same point. On December 13, 1967, not two weeks after the *Century* lost its name, observation car, and fast running, the *Broadway* was stripped of its all-Pullman status through combination with *The General*, had ten stops and 40 minutes added to its schedule, and lost *Mountain View* and *Tower View*. The mighty had truly fallen.

Other than PRR's and NYC's, the only one-railroad route between New York and Chicago belonged to the Erie, and its leisurely *Erie Limited*—Nos. 1 and 2, inaugurated on June 2, 1929, with economic Armageddon only months away—could offer primarily economy and scenery in its competition with the *Century* and *Broadway*. (Technically, the *Erie Limited* was a Jersey City, N.J.–Chicago train; connection to Manhattan was by Erie ferryboat to Chambers Street.) Late in the heavyweight era, when the Central and Pennsy flagships were making the New York–Chicago run in as little as 16½ hours, the *Erie Limited* needed about 24 for its journey. Actually, the *Erie Limited* never fully left the heavyweight era. The only lightweight cars Erie ever owned were 11 sleepers, purchased in three different lots. All coaches and diner-lounges ever operated on the *Erie Limited* and its running mates—the *Lake Cities*, the *Atlantic Express,* and the *Pacific Express*—in the streamline era were rebuilt heavyweights.

Though not a flyer, the *Erie Limited* did have its friendly charms—that plus splendid New Jersey and New York mountain scenery (including a delightful ride along the Delaware River), all seen in daylight in both directions. And the train did feature some handsome cars, including

LOWER RIGHT: In December 1957, A pair of Electro-Motive E8s leads the eastbound *Erie Limited* over the joint Nickel Plate-Erie swing bridge across the Grand Calumet River at Hammond, Ind. Though the train carried lightweight sleepers—the only true lightweight cars Erie owned—the coaches and diner-lounge were all modernized heavyweights. Following the 1960 Erie and Delaware, Lackawanna & Western merger, the *Erie Limited* became known as the *Erie-Lackawanna Limited*. GEORGE SPEIR

8-section compartment restaurant-buffet lounges *Ridgewood Country Club* and *Mahoning Country Club*. For years the train carried 8-section buffet-sun room-lounge cars, with deep windows in the observation end. And, since it was the premier and fastest train in the Erie fleet, it did command an extra fare for passengers traveling between Chicago and Passaic or Paterson, N.J., or New York City but not intermediate points. The *Erie*

RIGHT: The stately *Erie Limited* pauses at Binghamton, N.Y., on May 7, 1929. This train couldn't compete with either the *Broadway* or the *Century* in speed or amenities, but it had an easygoing charm and some fine scenery to offer. W. REUGGER, CAL'S CLASSICS COLLECTION

Limited and its kin survived Erie's 1960 merger with the Delaware, Lackawanna & Western, after which it was renamed *Erie-Lackawanna Limited*. In the mid-1960s, the train was rechristened again, receiving a famous DL&W moniker—*Phoebe Snow*—a name which Nos. 1 and 2 kept until their discontinuance in 1967. On January 5, 1970, the last vestige of former-Erie New York–Chicago service ended when Erie Lackawanna's *Lake Cities* concluded its final trips. At the time, regular rail travelers between Chicago and New York claimed that the *Lake Cities'* dining cars offered the best food of all on any train on any railroad between those points.

Baltimore & Ohio was another railroad determined to be a player in the Chicago–New York passenger sweepstakes. To do this, however, it needed help from the Reading and Central Railroad of New Jersey to move its through sleepers and coaches over the "Royal Blue Route" between Philadelphia—the eastern end of the B&O—and Jersey City, from which passengers were bussed and ferried across the Hudson to various drop-off points throughout Manhattan. B&O's *Capitol Limited* was arguably the premier Washington–Chicago service, going head-to-head with PRR's Washington section of the *Broadway* and later its Washington–Chicago *Liberty Limited*. B&O's New York service was essentially through cars from the *Capitol* and other trains, ferried east of Washington on separate Jersey City-bound trains.

Beginning in 1941 when the all-coach *Columbian* was extended to Jersey City and given a heavyweight consist that had been rebuilt in the streamlined mode for the *Royal Blue* in 1937, it received the Jersey City–Chicago chair cars. This practice continued when the train was re-equipped with lightweight cars (including domes) in 1949. Through cars also operated on the *Shenandoah*, on a later schedule than the *Capitol*, and on the less-illustrious *New York-Pittsburgh-Chicago Express* and *Chicago-Pittsburgh-New York Express* as well. Despite its efforts, the B&O exited the Chicago–New York market first when, in 1957, it ended all passenger service east of Baltimore and concentrated on what it did best: providing service between the Midwest and the nation's capital.

The Delaware, Lackawanna & Western was another carrier that offered New York–Chicago service with the help of partners. Its trains actually headed west from Hoboken, N. J., on the west shore of the Hudson, near Jersey City. The Lackawanna terminated in Buffalo, where it handed off its through cars to other carriers—primarily the Nickel Plate, but also the Michigan Central and Wabash. In the heavyweight era, Lackawanna operated four trains with Chicago sleepers: the *Lackawanna Limited*, *Chicago Limited*, *Western Special*, and *Whitelight Limited*.

In 1949 the railroad resurrected its great advertising icon, *Phoebe Snow*, the maid whose white dresses remained spotless because the railroad burned sootless anthracite, and inaugurated a stylish streamliner between Hoboken and Buffalo bearing her name. Westbound, *Phoebe* carried a New York–Chicago sleeper, handed over to Nickel Plate's *Nickel Plate Limited* at Buffalo. The *Westerner* was a joint DL&W-NKP operation between Hoboken and Chicago, with through sleepers and coaches. The *Westerner*'s eastbound counterpart was the *New Yorker*. After the Lackawanna merged with the Erie in 1960, the *Phoebe Snow* name was dropped, then, as mentioned earlier, revived and applied to the *Erie-Lackawanna Limited*—nee the *Erie Limited*.

The Lehigh Valley, an "anthracite road" like the Lackawanna, tapping eastern Pennsylvania's resources of hard coal, also operated Jersey City–Chicago and later New York–Chicago cars. (Beginning in 1918, LV trains ran into Pennsylvania Station.) The *Black Diamond*, LV's premier train, carried Chicago sleepers for a time, as did LV's *New Yorker* and the *Chicagoan*. However, these through cars were relatively short-lived, as LV's passenger services eroded faster than those of its competitors, and by 1961 the Valley had become a freight-only railroad.

Lehigh Valley, Lackawanna, Erie, Baltimore & Ohio: all these carriers played distinctly second fiddle to the Pennsylvania Railroad and New York Central. And, when all was said and done, Central was the virtuoso.

LEFT: Though the cover of this ***Capitol Limited*** **brochure from 1937 prominently features Chicago and New York as end points, the illustration is of Washington, D.C., sites, and the tag line is "The Road to Washington." In truth, the** ***Capitol*** **was a Chicago–Washington train with through cars to Jersey City (New York) handled by connecting B&O trains at Washington. WILLIAM F. HOWES JR. COLLECTION**

EPILOGUE

WHAT LITTLE REMAINS

On June 15, 2002, when the *20th Century Limited* would have celebrated its 100th birthday, the train that had set the standard for rail-travel luxury had been gone for almost 35 years—since December 3, 1967, when it vanished with a shocking suddenness and finality.

Its name, which was once a household word across the country, as often as not draws blank stares when mentioned today. It's tempting to lament that this "Greatest Train in the World" has vanished without a trace. But that wouldn't be quite true.

In early 1983, Amtrak's eastbound *Lake Shore Limited* runs along the Hudson River, following in the footsteps of the *20th Century Limited* but not in its grand tradition. This view is from the Bear Mountain Bridge, which served as a landmark-size "prop" for many photos taken of New York Central's Great Steel Fleet. HOANG CHI COOK

For one thing, there is Amtrak's *Lake Shore Limited*, a New York–Chicago passenger train that runs more or less on the *Century's* schedule and route—though hardly in its tradition. On the *Century's* centenary in 2002, the *Lake Shore* took 18 hours and 35 minutes to make the eastbound trek and 19 hours and 10 minutes for the westbound—a far cry from the 16 hours so proudly claimed for the *Century* in 1938, but better than the 20 hours that seemed such an accomplishment as late as 1929. (And much better than the 23 hours required for the Amtrak *Lake Shore's* eastbound journey early in its career.) In fact, as far short of *Century* standards as it falls, the *Lake Shore Limited* has been a success story for Amtrak.

Initially Amtrak's incorporators, mistakenly deciding that the system could support just one New York–Chicago service, selected the ex-Pennsylvania Railroad route through Pittsburgh. Thus at Amtrak's May 1, 1971, start-up, there was no passenger-train service between Chicago and Buffalo, though points east of there were served by Amtrak's continuation of Penn Central's "Empire Service" trains, which had been begun by NYC as part of the service reduction and realignment that killed the *Century*.

However, Illinois, Ohio, and New York quickly became the first states to exercise the 403(b) provision of the Amtrak law, which allowed states to institute service by providing (as originally stipulated) two-thirds of the needed subsidy, so on May 10 a New York–Cleveland–Buffalo–Chicago train entered service. For a name, Amtrak turned to a once-grand NYC train, the *Lake Shore Limited* (though initially not using "Limited" in the title), that had eventually fallen to decidedly secondary status. Amtrak left the unparalleled *Century* name to rest in peace—an appropriate decision, especially since the Amtrak *Lake Shore* had problems.

Though Amtrak was committed to relocating some of the better equipment from the West (where service and maintenance had survived at a higher standard in the last years of the private railroads than it had in the East), the *Lake Shore* ran largely with worn-out ex-Penn Central cars. An even greater problem was the failure of the participating states to cooperate fully on the train's operation and pay Amtrak any of the subsidy money promised, so on January 4, 1972, the train was abruptly discontinued, once again leaving Toledo and Cleveland without rail passenger service.

But on October 31, 1975, the run was reborn as the *Lake Shore Limited*, with through cars from Boston operating via Albany. This incarnation was the first annual "experimental route" to be designated by the Department of Transportation under a 1974 Congressional mandate. Almost immediately, the train became a success in terms of ridership. When, some two decades later, Amtrak's *Broadway Limited* was discontinued, the *Lake Shore Limited* became for a time the only New York–Chicago service. As of 2002, there were three New York–Chicago trains, but the *Lake Shore Limited* had become the premier run—ongoing timekeeping problems notwithstanding.

How else does the *20th Century Limited* live on? The Ben Hecht/Charles MacArthur play "Twentieth Century" is performed only rarely, but the musical comedy "On the Twentieth Century," which opened at New York City's St. James Theatre in early 1978, is mounted more often. This show, with music by Cy Coleman and book and lyrics by Betty Comden and Adolph Green (Broadway veterans all), is based on the Hecht/MacArthur play and, perhaps even more, the movie that followed.

Though the musical has a plot (a slim one, like its sources) and songs, singers, dancers, and actors, it was the title character—the Art-Deco gray, mauve, and chrome streamliner—that stole the show at the St. James. The audience was alerted right from the beginning that the train would be center stage, literally and figuratively. Barely had the conductor (the musical director, that is) raised his baton to start the flow of Cy Coleman's pleasant music (which at its best lilts with the cadence of clickety-clack) when steam suddenly exploded from the orchestra pit in accelerating bursts.

Robin Wagner, the show's designer, created a splendid streamliner on stage, one clearly emulative of Dreyfuss' 1938 train. The locomotive was a dead ringer for a streamlined J3a—even if it was a 4-6-0. The observation was an amalgam of Dreyfuss' round-end car and—in order to provide Imogene Coca, one of the show's stars, a perch to wave from—the open platform style of the heavy-weight era. The tailsign was very close to the famous Dreyfuss design that remained the train's signature for nearly 30 years. With its singing redcaps and sleek streamliner, "On the Twentieth Century" will recall a glamorous era and an irreplaceable train whenever it's produced.

The album cover for "On the Twentieth Century" features smart Art Deco graphics that reflect Robin Wagner's stylish scenic design. KARL ZIMMERMANN COLLECTION

Then there are small (not on-stage-size) replicas of pieces of the train—or even the whole thing. The J-class standard Hudson in various editions was perhaps the most noted of all of Lionel's creations. Lionel's 1937 J1e 5344, really a scale model rather than a toy, was the greatest. After World War II the company produced a semi-scale Hudson, and competitor American Flyer offered a New York Central Hudson as well. A model of the Dreyfuss Hudson is also available in HO scale.

Both the heavyweight and streamlined versions of the *20th Century* have been modeled in their entirety, perhaps never more dramatically than by photographer/artist Gerald Brimacombe, who fashioned a stunning O-scale replica of Dreyfuss' 1938 train from brass. After more than a year of research to ascertain the correct interior and exterior colors, he air-brushed on acrylic enamels that were created by Dupont by interpolating old paint formulas. Streamlined J3a Hudson 5450 was made in Japan.

And how about pieces of the real thing—cars that once served the *Century*, or the locomotives that hauled them? The well of locomotives comes up essentially dry. Sadly, not a single NYC Hudson survives,

The *Century* lives in miniature in Gerald Brimacombe's splendid model of Henry Dreyfuss' 1938 streamliner. The scene depicts a popular theme in NYC-related photos and art of eastbound and westbound *Century*s passing in the night. GERALD BRIMACOMBE

streamlined or non, nor a Niagara—the powerful, modern 4-8-4s that hauled Nos. 25 and 26 with some frequency in their latter years behind steam. (This stands in stark contrast to *Broadway Limited* motive power. K4 Pacifics, the steam locomotives most identified with the train, have been preserved, as have a whole bevy of GG1s, the rakish electric motors styled by Raymond Loewy that raced the *Broadway* between New York and Harrisburg, Pa.) A single New York Central Mohawk—a 4-8-2, which other lines would have called a Mountain, but not a railroad proud of its water-level route—survives: No. 3001, at the National New York Central Railroad Museum at Elkhart, Ind. Mohawks did haul the *Century* on occasion, so 3001 gets an honorable mention at least.

On the other hand, a very distinctive piece of *20th Century Limited* rolling stock not only survives but remains in regular service, and that is *Sandy Creek*, the glamorous observation car from the train's 1948 re-equipping. In May 1991, this car—which has passed through the purgatory of windowless, near-scrap-heap dereliction—reappeared as the tail car of the short-lived *American European Express*, then running between Chicago and New York as the *Greenbrier Limited* via the former Chesapeake & Ohio line through West Virginia's New River Gorge. Though the *AEE* made its last run in October 1991, sending the car back into temporary retirement, since 1994 it (along with the other *AEE* equipment) has been happily employed in the glamorous consist of the *American Orient Express*, a cruise train that ranges the length and breadth of North America. *Hickory Creek*, *Sandy's* twin, also survives. After a long career with Ringling Brothers/ Barnum & Bailey Circus, bringing up the rear of its Blue Train, the car is currently owned by the New Jersey-based United Railway Historical Society and is being refurbished.

In preparation for *AEE* service, *Sandy Creek* was completely rebuilt, with its interior configuration changed entirely. The forward section that once contained five double bedrooms was opened up and today is filled with over-stuffed swivel chairs and tables. There's a large bar in the middle. The round-end observation area, for so many years known by New York Central customers as the Lookout Lounge, remains the car's highlight. Now, in place of the original two steps, a ramp leads up to that raised area (currently six-inches lower than as-built). All the way to the rear, a tufted circular settee with a high back is topped by an extravagant bouquet of cut flowers. All around is a wonderful expanse of glass.

"The only thing original inside is the curved ceiling in the observation end," according to Eric B. Levin, the *AEE* official who supervised the car's $1.5-million rebuilding. The elegant new woodwork was done by Ethridge Cabinet Shop, and the upholstery and carpeting by Bay Point Interiors, run by Melissa Spann, wife of *AEE* owner William.

Now appropriately called *New York*, *Sandy Creek* looks smashing in *AOE's* livery of gold-banded cream and blue—a classic American streamliner paint scheme, though it owes its inspiration in part to Europe's Companie Internationale des Wagons-Lits, operator of the *Orient Express*. By all odds, the *American Orient Express* is the plushest train operating in North America in the twenty-first century. As such, it's the perfect owner for *New York*, nee *Sandy Creek*, which was the last grand gesture on behalf of the *20th Century Limited*, "The Greatest Train in the World."

When the United States Postal Service selected five trains— five locomotives, really—as subjects for its 1999 series commemorating great American streamliners, illustrated in watercolor by the late Ted Rose, the *20th Century Limited* and its Dreyfuss-styled Hudson were naturally at the top of the list— and the top of the pane of stamps. (Other trains included were the *Hiawatha, Super Chief, Daylight,* and *Congressional.*) The first-day-of-issue cover featured the *Century*, and the ceremony was held in Cleveland, a *Century* city. KARL ZIMMERMANN COLLECTION

ABOVE: To find the last remnant of the spirit and bones of the *20th Century Limited*, look aboard the observation car *New York* operated by the *American Orient Express*. This car began life in 1948 as the *Century's Sandy Creek*, and the Lookout Lounge remains a splendid window on the world for AOE passengers. KARL ZIMMERMANN

RIGHT: Though the interior has been vastly changed—gone, for instance, are *Sandy Creek's* five double bedrooms—*New York* retains an aura of elegance and luxury that *20th Century Limited* passengers would surely recognize. KARL ZIMMERMANN